# FROM GRACE TO GLORY

## MEDITATIONS ON
## THE BOOK OF PSALMS

# FROM GRACE TO GLORY:

## MEDITATIONS ON
## THE BOOK OF PSALMS

---

Murdoch Campbell

THE BANNER OF TRUTH TRUST

THE BANNER OF TRUTH TRUST
3 Murrayfield Road, Edinburgh EH12 6EL
P.O. Box 621, Carlisle, Pennsylvania 17013, U.S.A.

\*

© Copyright Murdoch Campbell 1970
First published 1970
Reprinted 1979

\*

ISBN 0 85151 028 0
Set in Monotype Baskerville 169
and printed in Great Britain by
Hazell Watson & Viney Ltd,
Aylesbury, Bucks

# Preface

While the whole of Scripture is unspeakably precious to the people of God, we believe that the Book of Psalms is one of their favourite spiritual pastures. Here, we find spiritual nourishment for our souls. In this Book we also have a mirror which reflects every aspect of true Christian experience – both our trials and our joys. Whatever depths of temptation or fear, or whatever height of consolation our lives may touch, we find these perfectly described in this wonderful Book. However distressing, or unusual, we may consider some of our own experiences to be, we find, in reading these Psalms, that men like David, Moses, Asaph, Heman and the others whose inspired lips sang these songs or uttered these prayers have, in other days, walked in the same paths as ourselves. Over the years – of what I hope I may call my own spiritual pilgrimage – I have often been sustained and comforted by the Lord applying to my soul words from these lovely infallible songs. Often have the words of David been present with me: 'Remember the word unto thy servant, upon which thou hast caused me to hope. This is my comfort in my affliction: for thy word hath quickened me.'

[Ps 119. 49–50]

And should these brief comments of mine bring a measure of comfort or edification to any of God's people I would consider that my labour was not in vain.

M.C.

RESOLIS,
ROSS-SHIRE

The figures used in the Psalm to describe both the godly and the ungodly man point to the real and ultimate difference between them. The one, in communion with God, with His Word in his heart and walking in His way, is stable, happy and fruitful. The other, driven by his own lusts and by every wind of false doctrine, is restless, helpless and lifeless. It was God's own hand that planted the godly man by the pure river of life. It was God's Spirit who quickened him so that all his well-springs might be in God alone. In the way of obedience to God's revealed will his peace is like a river, and his blessedness, or happiness, has the quality of variety and permanence. In this lower vale he shall continue to flourish by God's river 'which is full of water' – the river of truth and grace. His leaf shall not wither till he reaches the heavenly country where under an 'exceeding weight of glory' he shall come to full fruition and endless peace.

In this life the godly, or blessed, man is not immune from trials. Many are the storms which assail him here. But his roots are not of himself. The graces of the Spirit – faith, hope and love – are of God and, therefore, indestructible. 'Who shall separate us from the love of Christ?' A famous preacher once said that the dead tree often broke in the storm while the living tree, well nourished from hidden sources, withstood every storm, however severe and prolonged. Rooted and grounded in Christ the righteous shall endure to the end. The Psalm shows that the godly man is united to Christ in the totality of his nature. Mind, heart and will rest upon Him alone for salvation.

This first Psalm brings us to the very door of eternal

happiness – a happiness only the fringe of which we can touch here.

'The wicked are not so.' Unless they repent and return, the ungodly shall be driven by God's just wrath to endless woe. But let us listen to the sweet chimes of God's mercy toward a lost world. 'How often would I have gathered you.' 'And a man shall be an hiding place from the wind and a covert from the tempest, as rivers of water in a dry place, as the shadow of a great rock in a weary land.' The safety, promises and blessings of this Psalm are available to all who come to Christ for salvation.

### PSALM 2: KISS THE SON

One day I sat in a church. The minister gave out the second Psalm and the large congregation present began to sing:

> *Yet, notwithstanding, I have him*
> *To be my King appointed;*
> *And over Sion, my holy hill,*
> *I have him King anointed.*

As these words were being sung, *eternity* seemed to touch my spirit. What we call the 'time-barrier' seemed, for a moment, to dissolve. I felt I could see through the vistas of future ages. It was as if I had entered another world – a world of unspeakable peace. All the confusions, conflicts, noise and hatreds which distress our present world had passed away. All opposition to God in His moral rule, and in the government of His grace, had ceased. All hostile voices were for ever silenced.

There were one or two things which impressed themselves very deeply on my mind in that hour. One was the utter folly, wickedness, and impotence of men in their enmity against God. This Psalm speaks of the unity of evil forces which plot against the Lord and His Christ. As if millions of midges had by one consent resolved to blot out the sun! These, we notice, carry many high sounding names. They are 'kings', 'judges', 'rulers' and 'princes'. By modern categories they could be described as Atheists, Communists, Materialists, Humanists, or false Ecumenists. And as God watches their ways and listens to their words He just 'laughs'. There is, perhaps, no word in the Bible more terrible in its meaning and implications than this word. God has indeed often proved Himself to be 'terrible to the kings of the earth'. He 'laughs' because He knows that His Son, who has 'all power in heaven and in earth' could in a moment of time and by 'a little' exercise of His holy indignation wipe them out for ever.

The Psalm shows clearly that man, left to himself, is, consciously or unconsciously, an enemy of God. But set over against his hatred are God's forbearance and mercy. Though fallen and foolish, man may still be redeemed. God can give him a new heart and bless him with a new love. Man is also accountable to God. Hence His pleadings – 'Kiss the Son'; 'Be wise'; 'Be taught'; 'Lay down the weapons of your rebellion'.

That day as I sat in the house of God I knew that I was in contact with ultimate reality, and that the words of prophecy and promise will have their fulfilment in

God's own time. Let us, therefore, pray for the day when 'the wicked shall be no more', when all strife and opposition to Christ shall cease, and when the knowledge of the Lord shall cover the earth as the waters cover the sea.

PSALM 3: THE LORD OUR SHIELD

Sometimes, when we lie down to rest at night, our anxieties weigh more heavily upon our minds. The distractions and duties of the day may, in a measure, help us to forget them. But in the night, alone with our own thoughts, we become more conscious of our burdens. Yet here we have David, passing through one of the great crises of his life, lying down to sleep with God's peace and God's presence keeping his heart and protecting his life. This was the night when he crossed the brook Kidron. His enemies were bent on his destruction. In this cruel conspiracy they were led by Absalom, his foolish but well-beloved son. By human standards his plight was utterly hopeless. 'Many there be which say of my soul, There is no help for him in God.' In that hour he prayed and God heard him 'out of his holy hill'. These words mean that God blessed him with a promise that He would surround him like 'a wall of fire'. His angels would also encamp round about him as he closed his eyes in sleep, and the morning light would discover that all his enemies were brought low.

This Psalm, however, may be given a higher and a deeper application than what it has in its original context. All the people of God are waging war, 'not against flesh and blood, but against principalities and powers, against the rulers of the darkness of this world, against spiritual wickedness in high places'. These conflicts, fears and temptations may, as in the case of David, come upon us suddenly. In one hour, Satan, the great adversary, may invade our soul like a flood. We may feel helpless and full of fear. But – 'Call upon me in the day of trouble and I will answer you.' God will send help from above. His faithfulness to His unchangeable Word shall be our shield.

A man once retired to rest while he was in the grip of a great anxiety. He prayed that the Lord would renew to him His promise of His nearness and care. It was then that a voice seemed to whisper within his spirit: 'Wrap yourself up in the great promise of Psalm 91.' 'He that dwelleth in the secret place of the most High shall abide under the shadow of the Almighty. I will say of the Lord, He is my refuge and my fortress: my God; in him will I trust.' And for the rest of that night, and for many another night besides, his sleep was sweet to him.

The promise which God gave to Abraham belongs to all the children of faith. 'Fear not, Abram, I am thy shield, and thy exceeding great reward.'

'The Lord hath set apart him that is godly for himself'

One supreme end of God's choice of His people in Christ is that He might be their eternal Companion. These words show that God desires to have an holy converse with His people. He speaks to them and they speak to Him. Because He loves them with an everlasting love He will continue to communicate Himself to them for ever and ever. He has chosen the godly, or holy, man *for Himself*, both to glorify Him and to enjoy Him.

This converse with the Lord necessarily begins in this world of time. The Church speaks of Him as her Friend and Beloved who day by day upheld her in the way. Mary sat at His feet and John leaned on His bosom. By our new birth and adoption into His family, He stands in a new relationship to us. '*Now* are we the sons of God.'

This relationship, as we see in this Psalm, is the source of true spiritual joy. God renews our heart that He might dwell in our heart. When this happens we come to know the utter emptiness of all created things. We come to realize – in the words of the great Puritan, John Howe – that 'the creation is indigent'. 'Thou hast put gladness in my heart, more than when corn and wine doth abound with them.' The joy of the world is superficial and momentary. It does not touch our real selves and it does not extend beyond this world of time. The folly of man is that he loves 'vanity' or 'emptiness' and that God has no place in all his thoughts.

This joy of unbroken fellowship with God will be perfected in heaven. 'But I will see you again, and your heart shall rejoice, and your joy no man shall take from you.' Heaven is both a place and a state; but it is supremely the enjoyment of God. If this 'thirst' for eternal and full communion with God is within our souls, it is the earnest of our future bliss.

### PSALM 5: A WISE RESOLVE
'My voice shalt thou hear in the morning'

There are seasons in our life when, conscious of God's presence, we delight in the exercise of prayer. There are, sad to say, other times when we are given over to spiritual listlessness, and can say with one of the Puritans that a deep aversion to this duty is present in our hearts. Many may be our excuses for being remiss in the way of prayer. Some would say that the tasks of life are so numerous and so closely set to 'the wheel of time' that it is almost impossible to spend much time at the Throne of Grace. But David, though a ruler of a nation, and bearing many responsibilities, found time to pray. *'My voice shalt thou hear in the morning, O Lord; in the morning will I direct my prayer unto thee, and will look up.'* 'Time spent with God is no time lost.' It is time redeemed. It is time weaved into the context of eternity.

Prayer is our morning sacrifice. Since each day brings its own cares, we ought to begin the day by 'casting all our care upon him who cares for us.'

Prayer is a 'looking up' to God. We seek to set our affections on the things which are unseen and eternal, and to fix our gaze upon Him who is invisible. 'Turn thou away my sight and eyes from viewing vanity'. Lot was an heir of God, but we read that one day he lifted up his eyes and saw the cities of the plain. That one glance, which had its roots in a spirit of worldliness, cost him many a sigh in after days. But Abraham who stood beside him saw them not. Why? Because, subordinated to eternal realities, his eyes and affections were set on God and on that city that has foundations.

Prayer is often the arrow of the Lord's deliverance. This is the meaning of the word 'direct'. There are brief 'arrow prayers' which instantly reach the ear of God. We look up expecting an answer. Prayer is great only in its answer. 'Ask, and ye shall receive, that your joy may be full.' It is on this note that David's prayer ends. 'Let them that love thy name be joyful in thee.'

If we begin the day with God, as David did, we shall also end the day with His peace in our heart:

> *I will both lay me down in peace,*
> *And quiet rest will take,*
> *Because thou only me to dwell*
> *In safety, Lord, dost make.*

### PSALM 6: LOVE CONCEALED

One evidence of the Lord's love for us is that, for our sins and backslidings, He often brings us under the rod of correction. There is a promise that God will honour in the experience of His people in this world – 'As many as I love, I rebuke and chasten.' 'Whom the Lord loveth he chasteneth, and scourgeth every son whom he receiveth.' There are times, however, when we fear that His chastisement is the token not of His love but of His displeasure. Our sins, our indiscretions, and our wanderings out of His way, loom so menacingly before our own eyes that we cannot but fear that behind His chastisement lies His wrath.

In such days, and as we see in this Psalm, we have nothing to plead but His mercy. 'God be merciful to me a sinner.' David speaks of his weakness, his sorrow, his tears and his awareness of the loathsome disease of sin. But it is for mercy that he prays.

Yet, whatever the Lord may permit, there is – in the words of the saintly Archie Cook – 'not a drop of God's wrath in our cup.' He who stands behind the curtain of affliction is still our heavenly Friend. Christ bore the wrath and drank the cup of God's anger due to us for sin. And, although our cup may contain 'hard things' and 'the wine of astonishment', His love toward us is eternal and unchangeable. It is often in our pain that He reveals Himself as 'the brother born for adversity'.

The story is told of a good man, who through much fear and sorrow, remained in his bed on a Sabbath morning. And as he slept he dreamed. In his dream he found himself complaining to the Lord for His apparent lack of interest in him. It was then that he heard the words – 'I have graven thee on the palms of my hands; thy walls are continually before me.' When he awoke and looked at his hands he said, 'Well, I do not think I could forget a man if I had his name engraven there. I am only finite and God is infinite.' With that he arose and went to church, somewhat late. As he was walking in, the minister – the Rev. J. P. Struthers of Greenock – was reading from the Bible, 'I have graven thee on the palms of my hands'. Then he made the comment: 'Very possibly there are some here afraid that God does not care for them; I am certain there is at least one, and God's own answer to him is this – "I have graven thee on the palms of my hands." ' The man then realized that the hand which held the kindly rod of chastisement was the hand of Him who was nailed to the tree, and who loves His own to the end.

### PSALM 7: THE WISDOM OF THE SAINT
'My defence is of God'

It is, as we have seen, God's right and prerogative to chastise His own children. And only at their peril can a godless world or evil men touch those who are 'the apple of his eye'. In other ages He often warned both the powers of this world and ungodly individuals against doing His 'prophets' [or people] any harm. When they disobeyed His warnings, His agents of retribution often moved toward them on swift wings. This was true of such nations as Egypt, Edom and Babylon. It can also happen on the personal level. Although the final punishment of such men as Cush the Benjamite, of whom this Psalm speaks, is reserved till the Day of Judgment, God's displeasure may touch them in this world of time. This happened to the enemies of David.

What should be our attitude to those who misrepresent or persecute us, and who would scandalize

our name and character? As believers, we are commanded to love our enemies, to exercise patience and
to follow the example of Him 'who, when he was
reviled, reviled not again'. In certain circumstances it
may be needful to defend our name and character
from the false accusations of evil men. But there is a
more excellent and a wiser way.

David's method was to bring his trial to the Lord in
prayer, and to leave Him to vindicate his cause. An
old Christian minister used to give solemn instances of
how God sometimes, though not always, put to silence
lying tongues which maligned the righteous. This He
did by the hand of death, by the finger of time, by
solemn instances of His displeasure, and by unexpected
disclosures in His providence of where the truth lay.
'No weapon that is formed against thee shall prosper;
and every tongue that shall rise against thee in judgment thou shalt condemn. This is the heritage of the
servants of the Lord, and their righteousness is of me,
saith the Lord.' 'Commit thy way unto the Lord;
trust also in him and he shall bring it to pass; and He
shall bring forth thy righteousness as the light, and thy
judgment as the noonday.'

Does the universe speak to man of God's existence and glory? A great many people in this atheistic age would say 'No'. To them, creation supplies no proof that God is. As far as God is concerned the universe is to them like a lovely but an empty palace. But those whose eyes are blind, whose backs are to God, and whose minds and hearts are in the grip of prejudice and unbelief, cannot see Him in His works. Because of their aversion to the very idea of God they refuse the evidence of 'His wondrous works' which prove that 'His name is near'.

Creation speaks loudly to us of God's eternity and of His power and Godhead. Those who try to express in figures the age and magnitude of the universe are often lost in the mysteries of mathematics. They speak of millions of 'light years' and say they are still on the fringe of the great unknown, which goes to prove that although all things have a beginning, their ultimate cause or Creator is the eternal 'I AM'.

The universe speaks to us of God's power. By the word of His power all things came into being. In Him all things are sustained or 'held together', and when He so decrees, they shall all 'pass away'. The seal of His power is stamped on every star. Those who speak of creation as a 'spontaneous' or 'accidental' event are, by the use of such words, seeking a way of escape for their own sceptical minds.

How wonderful to think that all His works praise Him! We hear not their songs, but they reach His ear. And as we turn our eyes to 'the work of His fingers' we come to realize that He who called all the orbs of heaven by their names is also the God of peace. The

moon and the stars are indeed His lovely symbols of
tranquillity and peace.

> *He shall, while doth the moon endure,*
> *Abundant peace maintain.*

'What', in relation to the universe, 'is man'? Man is
the subject of God's love. Those who come to know
Him are nearer to His heart than all His works put
together –

> *Those that are broken in their heart,*
> *And grieved in their minds,*
> *He healeth, and their painful wounds*
> *He tenderly upbinds.*

> *He counts the number of the stars;*
> *He names them ev'ry one.*
> *Great is our Lord, and of great pow'r,*
> *His wisdom search can none.*

O the infinite condescension and love of God who
dwells with the poor and contrite in heart and with
those who tremble at His word!

The glory of God as revealed in all creation is nothing
compared to the glory which is manifested in the work
of redemption. This is 'the glory that excelleth'. Because of His love, revealed in the cross of Christ, millions
of the human race shall show forth His praise in the
world to come,

'And they that be wise shall shine as the brightness
of the firmament; and they that turn many to righteousness as the stars for ever and ever.'

To use a well-known phrase, man is ever 'trying to put himself on the map', and to give a favourable and impressive image of himself to his fellow-men. This is one of the fruits of his pride. By some achievement or deed he would perpetuate his own name. There are but few, however, who attain to 'immortality'. But if our so-called 'immortality' is rooted wholly within the context of time or of this world, it will fade away. If our so-called greatness stands unrelated to God, to His cause and to the true spiritual welfare of our fellow-men, it will perish. 'The name of the wicked shall rot.' Only the righteous man's memorial will prove everlasting. This is because the righteous man's prayer and desire are that the Lord alone may be glorified.

The vast majority of God's devoted people are unknown in this world. But they are not unknown in that fair world 'wherein dwelleth righteousness'. God has His 'Book of Remembrance' in Heaven, in which He records the deeds, the prayers, the conversation and the very thoughts of His people. Before an assembled universe He will recognize and disclose all that they have done for Him here. Do we wrestle with God in secret for a day of His power? Do we commend Him by our life and conversation? Do we love the gates of Sion and praise Him there? Do we seek by His grace and blessing to bring souls into His fold? If we do, we shall reap with joy. He will not forget our labour of love. What we do may be poor and unprofitable in our own eyes, but His promise is, 'Their works do follow them'. One day's work for Christ is worth a thousand years in the service of the world. Happy are they who can say with Job, 'My witness is in heaven and my record is on high'! This he said in deep humility with his head bowed.

Many years ago a poor, ill-clad and hesitant young man appeared in a pulpit. Apart from one poor man who invited him to his home, no one took any notice of him. Many years afterwards, when he had become a famous preacher, he appeared in the same church. After the service many plied him with invitations to become their guest. He remained silent, till he saw his old friend who had been so kind to him in the days of his poverty. Moving towards him he said that he would dearly love to become his guest for the second time. Let us take the matter to heart: 'I was a stranger and ye took me in.'

### PSALM 10: THE ETERNAL KING
'The Lord is King for ever and ever'

Once, when I was still a mere lad, I overheard a good man remark on what one of his friends in the Lord had said about God's essential nature. Nothing gave this man more consolation than God's unchangeableness. 'Jesus Christ the same yesterday, and today and for ever.' Some angels and all men have changed from their original state of perfection, but God cannot change. Not only is He without change in Himself, but He is unchangeable in His love, in His promises, and in His covenant faithfulness. We may sometimes fear that our evil hearts and thoughts may compel Him to withdraw

His mercy. This fear was in David's heart, too. 'Will the Lord cast off for ever? Will he be favourable no more? Is his mercy clean gone for ever? Doth his promise fail for evermore?' Let the Lord Himself answer these questions of a contrite soul. 'I am Jehovah, I change not. Therefore, ye sons of Jacob are not consumed.' How often I have thanked God that I overheard that remark by a true father in Christ! and that amid all my own fears, my deepest comfort also came from the same source!

Another precious recollection is that of sitting in a room with an old woman who is now, I believe, with God in the upper sanctuary. With great solemnity she repeated the words – 'From everlasting to everlasting, thou art God.' A thousand years in His sight are but as 'a watch in the night'. Generations, thrones and kingdoms rise and fall before His face; but 'thy throne, O God, is for ever and ever'. And because He lives, all His people shall be for ever established in His presence.

'The Lord is King for ever and ever.' Once I picked up a book in which I read of a Christian minister who was distressed in his mind because of the state of the world and of the apparent helplessness of the Church of Christ in the presence of prevailing iniquities. Then these words met his eye: 'The Lord doth reign.' Beyond and above all the floods of evil which were lifting their voice, he saw, by faith, a throne, and Him that sat thereon. Then he realized anew that all things were under the Lord's control and that nothing can happen without His permissive will. This Psalm speaks of the prevailing evils which so often bring fear to the hearts

of God's people. But when God's child fixes his eyes
on his eternal King he knows that all is well:

> *Let Israel in his Maker joy,*
>     *And to him praises sing;*
> *Let all that Sion's children are*
>     *Be joyful in their King.*

### PSALM 11: 'AN HORRIBLE TEMPEST'

There are few things more impressive and more awe-
inspiring than the prophecies of God's Word. Many of
these have had their fulfilment in the incarnation,
death and exaltation of the Messiah; and also in the
preservation of the true Church of God, and in the
history of nations. History is, indeed, His story. Not
only does prophecy deal with coming events in a
way that some may designate as predictable happenings,
or history repeating itself, but it often describes these
in detail. And these predictions are set in 'time contexts'
which sometimes stretch out to thousands of years,
and many of them indeed to the eternal world. If God
has in many instances infallibly fulfilled His Word in
the past, only the foolish would ignore what He says
with respect to the future. Those who fail to see that
an omniscient God is present in His own Word are
truly blind.

The solemn words of this Psalm were written long
after the destruction of Sodom and Gomorrah. Nothing
has yet happened in history like the tempest which is

one day going to descend on our world. There have certainly been great and devastating wars involving many nations. But for a wicked and unrepentant world, the worst is yet to be. The words of the Psalm, we know, have an ultimate meaning. They speak of God's wrath which shall remain for ever in 'the cup' or within the beings of evil men. Of this wrath they may get a foretaste on earth, 'for the wrath of God is revealed from heaven against all ungodliness and unrighteousness of men'.

And the wicked prepare all this for themselves. They condone and legalize the very sins which pave a way for God's indignation. Recently I listened to a preacher who said that the present Parliament has done more in a few years to undermine the moral foundation of the nation than any Parliament has done in the last three hundred years.

If a fearful night is awaiting all evil-doers, a lovely dawn is approaching for God's own people. 'The day is coming that shall burn as an oven; and all the proud, yea, and all that do wickedly, shall be stubble: and the day that is coming shall burn them up, saith the Lord of hosts, that it shall leave them neither root nor branch. But unto you that fear my name shall the Sun of righteousness arise with healing in his wings. . . .' As with the excellent General Booth, may our last hour here be 'a sunrise and not a sunset', an eternal calm, and not a storm never to abate.

'Help, Lord, for the godly man ceaseth'

We know of communities which were once blessed with men and women who, by their life and conversation, adorned the doctrine of God their Saviour. In such places one can recall the day when many of 'the godly', by their presence and prayers, graced God's house and maintained a true Christian witness both in their own churches and in their own homes. They were a people on whose spirits rested 'the dew of heaven'. Their very lives rebuked sin. They were also blessed with spiritual zeal and discernment.

David, in his own day, was surrounded by sad evidences of spiritual desolation through the departure of the godly. On all sides walked men of 'flattering lips' and of 'a double heart'. In the nation, and within the congregation of the Lord, men appeared who would wink at, and allow the grossest forms of evil. In modern language they were men of 'tolerance' and 'charity'. We have in this our own age many of their counterparts both in Church and State. In the opinion of such men even the grossest sins should be tolerated and condoned. And when such 'walk on every side, the vilest men are exalted' and praised.

What kind of help did David pray for in such a day? He prayed for the grace that would enable him to walk in the footsteps of those men who, in every age, walked with God and kept their garments clean. He prayed, especially, that God would raise up a seed who would serve Him in truth and holiness.

This indeed should be one of the subjects of our prayers in our own day. God's promise to His people has not yet reached its final fulfilment. It runs thus: 'I will pour my spirit upon thy seed, and my blessing upon thine offspring: And they shall spring up . . . as willows by the water courses. One shall say, I am the Lord's; and another shall call himself by the name of Jacob; and another shall subscribe with his hand unto the Lord, and surname himself by the name of Israel.' When, through the outpouring of the Holy Spirit upon all flesh, such men shall again appear among us, iniquity shall hide her face for very shame. How we should pray for the day when the Church of God in the world shall again become 'a joyful mother of children', and, in her warfare against evil, 'terrible as an army with banners'!

## PSALM 13: DOES THE LORD FORGET?
'How long wilt thou forget me, O Lord?'

There are seasons when we may fear that the Lord has forgotten us, and that He stands remote from our prayers. We may even fear, like David, that His apparent desertion or forgetfulness of us may be 'for ever'. But this cannot happen. His compassion flows toward us, we believe, even more tenderly in our trials than when our life is untroubled and our spirits are at ease. We may not be conscious of this, but His Word assures us that it is so. 'But Zion said, the Lord hath forsaken me, and my Lord hath forgotten me. Can a woman forget her sucking child, that she should not have compassion on the son of her womb? Yea, they may forget, yet will I not forget thee.' He has forgotten their sins. We remember them. We grieve over them. We pray like David:

> *My sins and faults of youth*
> *Do thou, O Lord, forget.*

Where are our sins? They are 'behind his back' and never will He look behind Him to discover any of them. 'I have blotted out as a thick cloud thy transgressions, and as a cloud thy sins.' These He will remember no more. Sometimes, as a boy, I used to watch the dark rain clouds which appeared over the sea near our home in the Outer Hebrides. Then the contents of these clouds would be poured out into the ocean until once more the sky was perfectly clear. Afterwards I heard these words being uttered in a prayer: 'Thou hast cast the sins of thy people into the sea of thy forgetfulness.' Sweet words! Through the merits of His dear Son God has forgotten our sins that He might for ever remember us in that love that passeth knowledge. Nor will the Lord forget His promise to His people! The word which He gives them is for ever 'settled in heaven', and that word He will magnify above all His name.

### PSALM 14: 'THE FOOL'

This Psalm presents us with a picture of man as he is, as he may live and as he may die. By God's standards and judgment, man in his sinful state is a born fool. He goes astray from the womb. His folly assumes many forms, both in his thinking and in his external behaviour. We may create a false image of ourselves and of one another, but God's description of us is the true one. He knows us as we are.

The Psalm reminds us that man is born a potential atheist: 'The fool hath said in his heart, There is no God.' By this denial of God he seeks to deny his own eternal existence. Natural death, he thinks, ends all. There is no God to whom he is accountable. Prayer, therefore, has no meaning. 'They call not upon the Lord.' Man is just a soulless animal. He can act as he pleases. In his permissive society he can revel on his dunghill till he becomes 'altogether filthy'. All sense of shame is banished from his mind. In the lower depths of his being – often called the sub-conscious mind – there is an enmity against God which manifests itself in his persistent ill-will towards God's people whom he would 'eat [or devour] as bread'. This poison proceeds from the fangs of the serpent which pierced through the soul of man in his fall. Whether we live in China, in Russia, or amid the rampant atheism and lawlessness of our own nation, this enmity against all who love God and who reflect His image often comes to the surface.

The most terrible moment in the experience of the men and women who are in the grip of such folly will be when, like the rich man in the parable, after death they lift up their eyes in hell. In hell there are no atheists. There they shall know that God is, and they shall remember their folly. 'Son, remember.' 'O that they were wise, that they understood this, that they would consider their latter end!' There will be millions in Heaven who were born with foolishness bound up in their hearts, but who, by God's grace, were made wise unto salvation. May we be found among them!

Once I lay in a hospital ward beside two elderly men. The one went on blaspheming the name of God; while the other, by his chaste conversation gave ample evidence that he was a new creature in Christ. Then I remembered the words, 'Then shall ye return and discern between the righteous and the wicked'. But only on the last Day shall we know how final and real that difference is.

PSALM 15: 'THE HEIR OF HEAVEN'

'He that walketh uprightly'

The man described in this Psalm stands in vivid contrast to the one spoken of in Psalm 14. Here the holy walk of the truly spiritual man is beautifully portrayed. The Psalm stresses the fact that to dwell with God demands true holiness of life. Such a life has its negative and positive side. There are things from which it refrains and there are things in which it engages.

The well-spring of an holy life is true righteousness before God. To dwell with God we must be clothed in the imputed righteousness of Christ and we must have an imparted righteousness of nature whereby we are renewed in the inner man. This twofold righteousness is reflected in our righteousness of life. 'Old things are passed away; behold, all things are become new.' This man is also in a new way: 'He walketh uprightly.' In his renewed heart is the treasure of truth. 'I have taken Thy testimonies as an heritage for ever.' His tongue is no longer a venomous, unruly member which back-bites or assails his fellow-men. His eyes look not with envy or unseemly interest on 'vile men'. Those who fear God are His companions. He refuses to change or to adapt himself to the fashion of this world, or to any teachings which are contrary to God's revealed mind. His money, honestly earned, never finds its way into the gambler's hand or into the hand of those who dishonestly pursue their crooked financial speculations. Dwelling in God's presence and in His tabernacle, he knows that within that tabernacle, as his rule of life, is the law of love which is the true expression of God's will. The ten commandments, he knows, had their origin in heaven. And love is the essence and fulfilment of that law. 'Thou shalt love the Lord thy God with all thine heart, and with all thy soul, and with all thy strength and with all thy mind; and thy neighbour as thyself.' There is nothing in the world more easy and more delightful than to honour God's law when His own love is in our heart. But without His love in our heart His commands are an intolerable burden. They are a pain and a crucifixion to the mere natural man.

A choice Christian man once said with regard to a departed friend, with whom he had worked and lodged for a number of years, that he had never heard him utter a word or do anything but which he felt could be traced to the grace of God which was in his heart. His holy life was the outward evidence of his love to God.

This 'Golden Psalm' is primarily Messianic. From all eternity Christ, who is the wisdom of God, had His delights with the sons of men. As the One from whom nothing can be hid, He knew the dread vale of humiliation, sufferings and death through which He must pass before any of His people could come to know and to tread the path of life, and to stand before Him in the fair world above. He must, in the likeness of sinful flesh, stand on this earth and 'taste death for every man'. For the joy set before Him He endured the cross and despised its shame. He tells us what this joy was to be. 'As the bridegroom rejoiceth over the bride, so shall thy God rejoice over thee.' By His resurrection from the dead He spoiled principalities and powers, and conquered death and the grave. To them He gave the irresistible command, 'Let my people go'. He emerged from the grave without seeing corruption. He ascended up into Heaven where, throughout eternity, He shall see of the travail of His soul and shall be satisfied.

God shows His people the path of life by convincing them, first of all, of their state of sin, misery and spiritual death. This is the work of His Spirit. Before they come to know the path of life, God gives them the sentence of death in themselves. They die to their own false hopes. It was the famous Dr John Kennedy of Dingwall who once said in speaking of his own conversion that the day of his death was, spiritually speaking, the day of his birth, and his marriage day as well. It was the time when his Lord passed by him and espoused him to Himself for ever.

In this life we sometimes enjoy sweet foretastes of

[31]

that fullness of joy which is awaiting us in God's presence. There are seasons when we can say 'My cup runneth over', and when God's presence fills our souls. I shall always remember two Christian ladies who, following a time of much consolation in God's house, could not conceal the joy that was in their hearts. The one, with her face radiating peace, repeated the words of this Psalm:

> *God is of mine inheritance*
> *And cup the portion . . .*

The other, with her eyes toward heaven, and with her hand on her heart, kept repeating the words: 'O the love of Christ!' While such drops from Heaven are sweet beyond words, not till we put off this our tabernacle shall our joy be full.

A Christian man once found himself in the grip of temptation and much fear. What if the evil thoughts which so often assailed his mind should follow him to eternity? It was then that a voice seemed to speak to him: 'In heaven you will be perfect in holiness and your soul shall be so full of God and of His love that there shall be no room for anything else within your being. Besides, you will be infinitely and eternally beyond the reach of sin and Satan and of all that distresses you here. Nothing can ever enter that glorious world that shall disturb the peace and happiness of God's people.' It was then with a good hope through grace that his soul danced for joy before the Lord.

'Thou hast visited me in the night'

When David uttered this prayer before God he was being spoken of by many in the nation as a deceitful man and an enemy of King Saul. But 'with a conscience void of offence' and with his heart and life open before God, he could, in all holy boldness, make his appeal to God at the throne of grace that he was innocent of their accusations. The great proof of his innocence, however, was that his soul enjoyed constant communion with God. If he regarded sin in his heart, the Lord, he knew, would not favour him with His presence. But the Lord was near to him; not only in the day, but in the night also he visited his soul in love and blessed him with 'a word in season'.

In several of the Psalms David mentions this converse with God 'in the night watches', 'when deep sleep falleth on men'. The Spirit of God who dwells in the hearts of God's children can, through the written Word, comfort them whether waking or sleeping. 'I sleep,' says Christ's bride in the Song, 'but my heart is awake.' 'He gives to his loved ones in sleep.' If these night visits are often mysterious, they are also solemn and memorable. Only an hour ago I was reading the words of one of the Puritan fathers, Pastor Thomas Jolly. 'One night,' he wrote, 'about this time I had such a dream as I could not but take much notice of. I was led along through a dark alley into a most sumptuous temple where I was unconceivably ravished in spirit, and was raised to sing part of the twenty-fifth Psalm, verses 5 and 6, in a tune unexpressibly melodious and in an exceeding high note, so that I seemed to have a taste of the angelic exercise and celestial state above.'

Like Samuel Rutherford, and many others of his contemporaries, God visited his soul in the night. Charles Haddon Spurgeon's comment on these words of David is worth repeating – 'We hope that we have had our midnight visits from our Lord, and truly they are sweet; so sweet that the recollection of them sets us longing for more of such condescending communings. Lord, if indeed we had been hypocrites, should we have had such fellowship, or feel such hungerings after a renewal of it?'

A Christian lady once visited our home in Resolis. She was downcast in spirit. She had no clear assurance of her faith or of her acceptance in Christ. In conversation she mentioned that one night, a little time previously, she awoke out of sleep with God's word on her lips – 'Thou art mine.' The words, she told us, brought a smile to her face, for they carried with them the flavour of heaven. We assured her that in this endearing promise God did claim her as His own, and that on His word, which can never pass away, she could rest her soul in peace.

PSALM 18: THE LIT CANDLE
'For thou wilt light my candle'

These are words of great literary beauty, but their spiritual meaning is lovelier by far. This Psalm, which is also to be found in 2 Samuel, chapter 22, marked David's deliverance from his prolonged season of trial and persecution. The dawn of a better day had arrived. What interpretation can we legitimately give these words?

Solomon, David's son, speaks, for example, of the spirit of man being the candle of the Lord. When, by God's Spirit, we are called out of darkness into light, a candle is lit within us that shall never go out. We are then enlightened in the knowledge of Christ. The soul which has lain so long in the shadow of death becomes light in the Lord. The eyes of our understanding are opened and with all the saints we see by faith the things which are unseen and eternal. 'The path of the just is as the shining light which shineth more and more unto the perfect day.'

To all who are thus enlightened God gives the candle of His promise. David, like Abraham and many other of the saints, could remember the day when God gave them His Word of promise. And like them, the wistful hope might have remained with him for a season that his candle would continue to shine constantly and peacefully to the end. But it was not so. God cannot break or withdraw His promise to His people, but He may try them in their faith in His promise. In his day of distress Job could remember when God's candle shined on his head and when the secret of God rested upon his tabernacle, but in one hour dark clouds of trial descended on his life, as if his candle had gone out for ever. But God turned his captivity and honoured His servant.

Is there not also the candle of God's providence? God's providence, as we know, can be a great deep. 'Thy way is in the sea and thy path in the great waters, and thy footsteps are not known.' As these dark hours emerge in our life we say with Jacob, 'Against me are all these things'. Only in eternity shall we fully know what the end of the Lord is in all that He allows in our life here. He will then light our candle and make us see that all things did work together for our good. In David's own words, that day 'shall be as the light of the morning . . . even a morning without clouds'.

Such days of trial are often associated with what we call spiritual desertion. We say with the Church, 'Saw ye him whom my soul loveth?' Clouds take Him out of our sight. We mourn over the apparent absence of the One who said, 'Lo, I am with you always'. 'I will never leave thee, nor forsake thee.' No, the candle of His presence shall never wholly go out in our souls. Very soon we shall come to the end of our pilgrimage journey here, but our candle of hope will not fail us in the last dark vale. 'The righteous has hope in his death', for he has the oil of grace in his soul. His hope shall not be put to shame, because the love of Christ is shed abroad in his heart. The candle of grace will continue to burn till we reach the land of glory where we shall 'need no candle, neither light of the sun, for the Lord God giveth them light, and they shall reign for ever and ever'.

One lovely summer evening as I stood with an older and somewhat downcast friend outside a church, an elderly lady from Gairloch in Ross-shire approached us, and in a soft voice repeated these words:

> *For all those that be righteous*
> *Sown is a joyful light . . .*

I could see these words touched my friend's heart and filled him with joy.

There is also the candle of our Christian witness. Let us pray for grace that our light may shine before men 'till the day dawn and the day star arise in our hearts'.

A Christian man once told the story of a very godly, but a very timid man who, on his death-bed, was full of grief. He had never confessed his Lord in public. As he lay dying, the Lord, by His Word, assured him that his place in heaven was prepared, and that a welcome awaited him at His door. But He also reminded him that if, like him, all His people in that community had failed to confess His name, before men He would have been left without a witness there. At this the dear old man wept, until he went to the place where there are no more tears.

PSALM 19: THE CONVERSION OF THE SOUL

'The law of the Lord is perfect, converting the soul.'

There are varieties of Christian experience. This is true, especially, with regard to our soul's conversion. But there is one place where we all meet. In our conversion God's Spirit uses His Word as the supreme means of bringing us to Christ. In some cases His voice may speak to the soul directly and without any human instrumentality. In most cases, however, He blesses the preaching of His Word through His own witnesses. In the cases of Abraham and Paul, God's voice came directly from heaven, but in the case of the thousands

who were brought into His kingdom on the day of
Pentecost, the Word was blessed through one of His
apostles. Some of those who followed our Lord in the
days of His humiliation, did so by His own direct
command – 'Follow me'. Others came through the
words of those who had come to know Him and who
would have others share their blessings.

It is true also that some come to their spiritual rest
through much fear and concern. They are brought to
'the mount that might be touched' and from the height
of which they hear God's holy law sealing, as it were,
their damnation. They tremble under a burden of
conscious guilt: 'Cursed is everyone that continueth not
in all things which are written in the book of the law
to do them.' But there is not only an awakening word,
but a word of reconciliation as well: 'Behold the Lamb
of God who taketh away the sin of the world.'

If such men as Paul and John Bunyan could trace
the beginning of their spiritual pilgrimage to the dread
hour when God spoke to their soul in the accents of
His law, there were others like Nathanael, Mary of
Bethany and Lydia who were drawn to Him by the
still small voice of His love: 'I have loved thee with an
everlasting love.' If, like Paul and Bunyan, many could
afterwards rejoice in their 'time of love', those who
came in gently by the door of His love also had their
testings and siftings soon enough.

In the conversion of some, God moves in a mysterious
way. Recently I read the story of a Hebridean sailor
who almost drank his way to a lost eternity, and whose
Bible – his mother's gift – lay untouched in his bag
year after year. One night as he went to bed he dreamed.

He dreamt that he was present in the church of his boyhood days, and that a good man present repeated with great solemnity the words of the second Psalm. When he awoke, the words were audible within his spirit:

> *Kiss ye the Son, lest in his ire,*
> *Ye perish from the way,*
> *If once his wrath begin to burn:*
> *Bless'd all that on him stay.*

This was his 'hour of destiny'. From that moment he began to seek 'the city which hath foundations'.

As the Psalm speaks of the converting power of God's Word, it also tells us what are the fruits of such a conversion. We are 'made wise unto salvation'. We receive the 'end of our faith, even the salvation of our souls'. We 'rejoice in God's Word as those who find great spoil'. By God's Word our eyes are 'enlightened'. 'We, beholding as in a glass the glory of the Lord, are changed into the same image from glory to glory, even as by the Spirit of the Lord.' Our lives become progressively 'clean'. We are enabled more and more to die unto sin and live unto righteousness. We acknowledge that God is just and righteous in all that He says and in all that He does. The Psalm also 'warns' us against 'presumptuous sins' on which many have made shipwreck. These, by His grace, we seek to avoid. But beyond all, we value 'the great reward' awaiting all who keep and obey His Word – 'Fear not Abram; I am thy shield and thy exceeding great reward'. Christ, the Pearl of great price, is the treasure of all the saints.

'The name of the God of Jacob defend thee'

Although the name 'Jacob' in this verse may mean the race of Israel, we could give the word a personal application. God's relationship with His people is intimately personal. He is the God of Abraham, of Isaac and of Jacob. 'This is my name for ever and my memorial unto all generations.' It was at Bethel that Jacob had his most wonderful experience of God's covenant love to him. When afterwards He appeared to him He said: 'I am the God of Bethel', that is, the God whose tabernacle is with men. To Jacob, this name was precious beyond words. All his life he remembered that night when, journeying to an unknown country, he rested his weary head on a stone and slept. It was then that the eternal world disclosed its greatest mystery to his soul. He saw, in a type, the glorious One who was to unite heaven and earth, the eternal and incarnate Son of God. He saw the angels of God ascending and descending upon the Son of Man. It was there that the awe of God's presence solemnized his spirit – 'How dreadful is this place'. There God blessed him and gave him His promise of preservation in this world and an happy eternity with Himself. Some twenty years after this hour of communion at Bethel, God reappeared to him. It was a time of great fear and crisis. He had separated himself from his loved ones, and had crossed the brook Jabbok. Esau, his earth-bound brother, was coming towards him. He anticipated the worst. But a prayer that was born of anguish reached the ear of God. Then it happened. A 'man' wrestled with him till the break of day. The God of Bethel! The Angel of the Covenant! 'He had power with the angel and prevailed.' 'And he blessed him there.'

It is interesting to note that his hours of greater nearness to God came to Jacob when he was alone and in much anxiety. Christ is with His own in 'the day of trouble'. In retrospect, Jacob knew that his life was, moment by moment, upheld by his God. He spoke of Him as 'the Angel who fed him', who led him and who kept him all his days. His last speech on earth included the words, 'I have waited for thy salvation, O Lord'. Blessed are the people who have the God of Jacob for their refuge and portion!

### PSALM 21: LIFE DESIRED AND GIVEN
'He asked life of thee and thou gavest it him'

Christ is before us in this Psalm in His eternal glory and as the only Mediator between God and men. As God, He had no need of the gift of life, for in Himself He is the ever-living I AM, 'in whom dwelleth all the fullness of the Godhead bodily'. He is the source and sustainer of all existence and the fountain of life and blessedness.

But in this Psalm He is before us in His mediatorial office, asking the Father to give Him life – not for Himself, but for those who had, because of their sin, lost communion with God and had, therefore, no life. Sin pays its dread wages to all mankind. 'For the wages of sin is death.'

God gave Christ His request. He gave Him a fullness of life, of truth and of grace, which He communicates to all who believe on His name. The 'blessing is on the head of Joseph and on the top of the head of him who was separate from his brethren'. He was given the Holy Spirit without measure. This blessing remained not on His own head. It went down to the skirts of His garments, or in other words, reached the whole of His mystical body, the Church:

> *Like precious ointment on the head,*
>   *That down the beard did flow,*
> *Ev'n Aaron's beard, and to the skirts,*
>   *Did of his garments go.*
>
> *As Hermon's dew, the dew that doth*
>   *On Sion's hills descend:*
> *For there the blessing God commands,*
>   *Life that shall never end.*
>
> [Ps 133]

Out of Christ's fullness the new-born babe receives grace upon grace. The well-springs of the soul are in Him alone. The faith which is implanted in the soul is born of need and is therefore a receptive, dependent grace.

'It is more blessed to give than to receive.' We cannot conceive of the joy which this bestowal of life gives to Christ. He rejoices in the salvation of His people. There was music and dancing in the father's house when the prodigal son returned home. Not because he brought anything with him into that home apart from his sin and his needs! The joy of the home sprang from the fact that he was now restored to God and in possession of eternal life. 'This my son was dead and is alive again.'

Those who receive this life long for the day when they shall neither hunger nor thirst any more, and when their praise of Him shall be perfect. They look for the day when His promise of more abundant life shall be fulfilled.

It was Samuel Rutherford who once remarked that he was sailing to heaven in the ship of promise, and that he longed for the day when she would sink for ever in the ocean of God's love.

### PSALM 22: HIS LOVE REMEMBERED

'All the ends of the earth shall remember and turn unto the Lord'

A famous Christian thinker once said that if men would retire to a quiet place for but one hour and seriously ask themselves certain questions related to their life and destiny, it would be worth years of thoughtless bustle and foolish distraction. What is man? For what end did God create him? Is he any more than a fallen creature involved, apart from God's intervention, in an eternal tragedy? Does physical death end his existence? Is there a world to come and a God whom we must one day meet? Is the Gospel, as some would tell us, relevant to man's eternal welfare? Such questions are both solemn and imperative; but not two in a thousand go aside to ask themselves such questions. Alas! sin, which is a deception, a distraction and a disease, has dominion over them. Satan, who is the god of this world, has blinded their eyes and is continually, and often successfully, working to direct their thoughts from God, His Word and their own perilous state.

Although the Cross of Christ, of which this Psalm speaks, is a supernatural revelation of God's love to men, it is largely ignored. Although it is God's full and final answer to man's perplexities and needs, men still look upon it as 'foolish' and irrelevant to their needs and happiness.

We are living in an age which has largely forgotten God. 'God is not in all their thoughts.' Few there are who stand amazed and enraptured before the Cross which proclaims the love of God to a fallen world.

The pages of history, however, tell us of times, places and people who in other days did remember God's love in sending His Son into our world to bring us to Himself. In retrospect there is the glorious apostolic age, the period of the Reformation, the great evangelical revivals by which multitudes were brought into God's kingdom through the preaching of the Cross. There is still in this age of forgetfulness of God 'a remnant' who remember God's mighty works, and who know that it is when we preach and direct men to the Lamb of God that the Holy Dove, God's Spirit, descends upon us.

But the best is yet to be! The day is coming when 'all the ends of the earth' shall look to God, and when the shout of a King shall be heard among the nations of the earth. Jews and Gentiles shall look to Him whom they have pierced. Their Bochim shall be followed by a Bethel. 'The Lord is there.' The evils, the blasphemies and the degenerate 'enjoyments' of a godless age shall be forgotten like a weird dream.

Meantime let us pray, 'Thy kingdom come: Thy will be done in earth as it is in heaven'.

### PSALM 23: 'HE RESTORETH MY SOUL'

It is agreed that David composed this Psalm when, as a youth, he tended his father's flock. The Psalm is a perfect portrayal of the relationship between the shepherd and his sheep, especially in the oriental world. But David lifts his theme into the higher realm of the tender relationship between the Shepherd of Israel and those who are under His care.

Where, in the experience of God's people, do we begin with these words which speak of the divine restoration? Is it not a restoration from death to life? 'You hath he quickened who were dead in trespasses and sins.' God's Word reminds us that 'she who liveth in pleasure is dead while she lives'. 'This is life eternal, that they might know thee the only true God, and Jesus Christ whom thou hast sent.'

He restores our soul also into 'the paths of righteousness'. The living man walks in a new and living way. 'And an highway shall be there and a way, and it shall be called the way of holiness. The unclean shall not pass over it; but it shall be for those; the wayfaring men, though fools, shall not err therein.' When Christ's Bride asked her Beloved where she might enjoy the fare and the rest of His flock, He commanded her to

go forth 'by the footsteps of the flock' – the way of
truth and holiness – in which all His people have
walked from the beginning of time. 'The ways of the
Lord are right, and the just shall walk in them.'

There is also a restoration from destitution to fullness.
'My cup is full and running over.' 'My table thou
hast furnished.' They feed in green pastures and by
still waters. It was this realization that led the wayward
son to his happy resolve to return to his old home
where there was 'bread enough and to spare'. 'He
feedeth his flock like a shepherd.' Although, like
Israel of old, their way home is through a 'great and
terrible wilderness', they eat daily of the hidden manna
and drink of the river of God's pleasures.

The Lord's people are also restored from restlessness
to peace. 'He maketh me to lie down.' 'I will give you
rest', is Christ's great promise to all who follow Him.
'As the beast goeth down into the valley, the Spirit of
the Lord caused him to rest.' Their faith in His Word,
and in His love and power, gives them peace of mind
amidst all their conflicts. They are kept by His power,
and their lives are hid with Christ in the very bosom
of God. Therefore they fear no evil. While they are
here, goodness and mercy shall follow them.

David anticipates the day when, in the Eternal Home,
all shall be well. He who has been the dwelling place
of His people in all generations shall bring them all
into His fold to enjoy 'the rest which remaineth to
the people of God'.

The contrast between our Lord's entrance into our fallen world in our nature and His return to the heavenly world after He had accomplished His work is truly awe-inspiring. Apart from the few to whom this glorious secret was at the time revealed, His first coming was unknown and unobserved. Angels did indeed announce His coming, but only to a few. No earthly palace was prepared for Him. He lay in a manger, tenderly nursed by the one who 'kept in her own heart' the great secret of the mystery of godliness, God manifest in the flesh.

He came to redeem His people. No one else could have done this. He had surveyed the universe to see if there was any other who could have rescued them from their plight. 'And I looked and there was none to help: and I wondered that there was none to uphold: therefore mine own arm brought salvation unto me; and my fury it upheld me.' Death, sin and all the powers of darkness held them in their dread sway. The powers of evil are such that only God Himself could overcome and destroy them. His day of vengeance was also His day of victory. His resurrection and exaltation testified that He had procured eternal salvation for His people.

From the slopes of Bethany Christ ascended into heaven. As He entered in through the everlasting doors angelic hosts and 'the spirits of just men made perfect' sang for joy. The Conqueror is Home and He is not alone.

One of my old college professors used to speak about those many saints in Jerusalem who through the death and resurrection of Christ emerged from their graves. 'And what,' the dear man would ask, 'happened to those saints? Did they return to their graves? No, they went into heaven with Christ.' They formed, as it were, the first sheaf of that great harvest which He is to reap at the end of time. 'He shall see of the travail of His soul and shall be satisfied.'

There are also those who, legitimately and properly, give these words a subjective interpretation. The soul of man is immortal. But in a state of sin, man's soul is occupied, and the door is shut against the One who would come in. Happy are they who, in obedience to His Word say, 'Come in, Thou blessed of the Lord'. While we know on the one hand that 'it is God who worketh in us both to will and to do', the relationship, on the other hand, between the overtures of God in the Gospel and man's response to His overtures, is too solemn and mysterious for human reasoning. But there is no conflict between the two truths. Therefore, Christ's last word to all who keep the doors of their heart closed against Him will be – 'I was a stranger and ye took me not in'.

And what a blessed day it will be when we shall pass through the everlasting doors above to go no more out. An elderly Christian woman once sat by the bed of a dying girl who had given ample evidence that she knew the Lord. Their last words together were a verse from a Psalm: 'O set ye open unto me the gates of righteousness: Then will I enter into them, and I the Lord will bless.'

'The secret of the Lord is with them who fear him; and
he will show them his covenant'

There are, as we know, degrees of friendship among
men. There are, for example, those who sometimes
cross our path, but of whom we have little or no knowledge. There are also those with whom we may discuss
things that concern our earthly life, but who may be
strangers to our inward Christian experiences. And
there are the few who, in their spiritual sympathy and
knowledge, come nearer to us than any other. To such
we may wisely unbosom ourselves. They understand
us in our trials and in our spiritual enjoyments. If this
is true of the intimate link between individual believers,
how much more of the tender and unbroken relationship between the Lord and His people! The word
'secret' in this Psalm has this lovely meaning. God and
His people share their secrets with each other. He opens
His heart to us. He gives us an assurance of His love,
a sight of His glory, and often a 'word in season' from
His mouth. When He sees fit He may unveil certain
events in His holy providence which stand related to
the future. These disclosures may apply to ourselves,
to other believers, or to the world in which we live.
All this He does by His Word and Spirit. As it is His
glory to conceal a thing, it is His glory also to reveal
His 'secret' to His saints. 'Shall I hide from Abraham
that thing which I do?' 'Surely the Lord God will do
nothing, but he revealeth his secret unto his servants
the prophets.'

There are those who question and even disparage
this intimate converse between the believer and God
as a species of unwholesome mysticism. As if there

[49]

could be any true Christian experience without this intimate communion between God and the soul of man!

The Psalm tells us that the covenant of grace is God's great revelation of His lovingkindness to His people. This is that 'better covenant' which He made with all His people in Christ, who is its Mediator. Whatever perplexities touched the life of David, He was assured that God had made an everlasting covenant with Him in the Son of His love. It was a covenant which was 'ordered in all things and sure'.

> *Blessings on blessings through ages unending,*
> *Covenant fullness in glorious flood:*
> *Ours is a hope which no mortal can measure,*
> *Brought in by Jesus and sealed in His blood.*

The people who share the secret of the Lord are a people who fear Him. This is a fear which is wrapped up in love and reverence towards His name. It is a fear which is ever seeking greater nearness to Him and which, in all things, seeks to be reconciled to His will. It is the fear of the true-born child, and not, as Paul describes the ungodly, of 'the bastard'. Evil men may be afraid of God, but their voice is – 'Depart from us, for we desire not the knowledge of thy ways'.

PSALM 26: GOD'S HOUSE LOVED
'I have loved the habitation of thy house'

The love of God in the soul reveals itself in many ways. It goes up to Him 'who first loved us'. It goes outward

to all His people – 'Thy people shall be my people'.
It also embraces every syllable of God's written Word.
'O how love I thy law! It is my meditation all the day.'
And again, it is devoted to God's house 'where his
honour dwelleth'. How tenderly does David express
his deep affection for God's house in other Psalms! In
the day when he was excluded from the tabernacle he
envied the birds which could rest quietly, or build their
nests, in its remote corners. 'My soul longeth, yea, even
fainteth for the courts of the Lord.' His prayer on earth
was that he might dwell in God's house for ever. God's
own presence in the place 'where he desires to dwell' is
often the foretaste of heaven to His people.

Often have I envisaged the large congregation which
many years ago ended their open-air summer service in
a quiet Highland vale with the words – 'Arise, O Lord,
into thy rest; Thou, and the ark of thy strength'. God's
presence was among them, and as they dispersed to
meet again in the nearby church these words were
their prayer, their praise and desire. And there, indeed,
He did tarry for many days.

A minister of the Gospel once told of a woman in
his congregation who was totally deaf, but who was
never absent from God's house. 'Though I cannot hear
you,' she said to him, 'I come to God's house because
I love it; for there I am in the more immediate presence
of God and among His people, who are the honourable
of the earth.'

In another congregation there was an old man who
was brought to the Lord late in life. His love for God's
house became a marked characteristic of his life. He
lived in the days when there were no conveyances and

when most people had to walk to church. One day, during which the skies had poured down a deluge of rain, he appeared at the church door. Few had ventured out. To a friend, who expressed surprise at his coming out in such weather, he said, 'I came here today because every valid excuse as to why I should not come was taken away'. With the Psalmist he could say:

> *How lovely is thy dwelling place,*
> *O Lord of hosts, to me!*
> *The tabernacles of thy grace,*
> *How pleasant, Lord, they be!*

These were the spiritual contemporaries of David, and of God's true saints in every age.

This deep spiritual attachment to God's house implies a complete and final separation from the abodes of godless people, whether they meet at whist drives, in the bingo or dance hall, or in 'places of worship' where God is unknown. 'I have not sat with vain persons, neither will I go in with dissemblers. I have hated the congregation of evildoers, and will not sit with the wicked . . . Gather not my soul with sinners.' These words tell us that neither in this world nor in the world to come do God's people desire communion with any but Himself and those who love Him.

PSALM 27: 'THE BEAUTY OF THE LORD'

When David spoke of his love for God's house he was aware that his affection for the house was derived from his love to God Himself. This love was so deep and permanent that in order to behold the beauty of the One whom he loved, he would dwell in His house for ever. This is, indeed, a desire which is present in every gracious soul. It is also a desire which has its measure of fulfilment in this life. 'We beheld his glory.' It is the glory of Him who is 'the root and the offspring of David and the bright and morning star'. Even the glimpses we get of Him here truly ravish the heart. The bride in the Song speaks of Him as 'altogether lovely'. 'My Beloved is white and ruddy, the chiefest among ten thousand.' 'Thou art fairer than the children of men.' When the wise men saw His star – the symbol of His eternity and glory – 'they rejoiced with exceeding great joy' – 'joy unspeakable and full of glory'.

In the whole of His being, God is the essence of perfection and beauty. Each of His attributes has its own peculiar loveliness. 'God is a Spirit, infinite, eternal, and unchangeable, in His being, wisdom, power, holiness, justice, goodness and truth.' These precious words are not an exhaustive definition of His being; they touch but the fringe of His glory:

> *God's mighty works who can express,*
> *Or show forth all his praise?*

Here we see Him but darkly through a glass; but one day we shall see Him as He is.

Has this miracle of enlightenment taken place in our own lives? Are we among those of whom Christ spoke on earth: 'I thank thee, O Father, that thou hast hid these things from the wise and prudent and hast revealed them unto babes.'

An old earthbound man one day sat in a church in Ross-shire. For the first time in over sixty years he was arrested by a message which proclaimed the beauty of Christ. A new and wonderful light flooded his mind. The One who had been but a mere remote name to him all his life disclosed Himself to his soul. The inner eyes were enlightened. From that hour he was a new man. The Bible became a new book; he had entered a new world. In God's house he had seen the King in His beauty.

It was Moses, who 'wist not that his face shone' after a season of near communion with Jehovah, who also prayed, 'And let the beauty of the Lord our God be upon us'. Those who behold His glory are changed into the same image by the Spirit of the Lord.

PSALM 28: 'THE OPERATION OF HIS HANDS'

One proof of man's spiritual depravity and blindness is seen in his indifference to God's works. The Bible reminds us that His works reveal that His name is near. We are commanded to think of these. 'The works of the Lord are great, sought out of all them that have pleasure therein. His work is honourable and glorious.'

Man himself is one of God's masterpieces of creation. He is, in fact, the crown of creation. He was made in the image of God. 'I am,' said the Psalmist, 'fearfully and wonderfully made.' Because God breathed His own breath into man's being he must necessarily exist for ever. It was this act that imparted immortality to his being – whatever arguments he may put forth to the contrary. And man has an instinctive awareness of his own immortality for he cannot conceive of himself as 'not being'. The theory of evolution as it stands related to man is foolish. Whatever physical similarities may be discovered between man and other creatures, the moral, intellectual and spiritual distance between them is almost infinite and, as far as this theory goes, unexplainable. The awe-inspiring phenomenon of conscience, for example, is one evidence of our accountability to God. It proclaims that one day, unless we are forgiven, our sin will find us out.

But man is not what he was as God created him. Sin has inflicted such appalling damage upon his being that he is now a spiritual and moral wreck. Left to the freedom of his own will, with his eyes open, and contrary to God's warning, Adam walked into Satan's snare. But by grace man can be reclaimed. God is able to change him into a new being. Oh! how we should admire God in this work. The conversion of a soul is truly a work of God which should command our interest and fill us with wonder.

During my lifetime I have seen thousands of men and women in whom this great work has been wrought. Some of them were men and women whom one, without exaggeration, could describe as low and degraded, changed into new beings in one hour. How did it happen? They all have a testimony to give: 'Come and hear, all ye that fear God, and I will tell what he hath done for my soul.' What answer has an infantile psychology to spiritual conversion? None! It

[55]

is something utterly beyond its reach. It cannot explain it, though it tries to explain it away.

There is another work of God which man should admire and regard above all others. It is Christ's work of redemption. In this work we have a glorious display of God's love, wisdom and power without parallel in the universe. If we regard not this work of God we close in our own face the only door leading to everlasting happiness. It is in this work that we see into the very heart of God.

God's glory and power stream toward us also in the works of creation and providence. 'The heavens God's glory do declare.' 'Consider the lilies how they grow.' The birds which warble in the sky sing because God blesses them.

Do we regard the works of God? Can we say:

> *Were the whole realm of nature mine,*
> *That were an offering far too small,*
> *Love so amazing, so divine,*
> *Demands my soul, my life, my all.*

If not, what is the alternative? 'Because they regard not the works of the Lord, nor the operation of his hands, He shall destroy them and not build them up.'

PSALM 29: THE 'STILL SMALL VOICE'

In its natural setting this Psalm derives its vivid imagery from one of those somewhat terrifying storms which, at certain seasons, passed over the land of Palestine.

David could hear its first remote peals over the distant hill of Hermon. Within an hour its thunders would pass over the place where he sheltered. Then its voice would lessen till at last, far away above the sea, its last rumblings would give way to a perfect stillness and peace. To the Psalmist the storm was not merely the voice of nature. It was the voice of God.

The Psalm is an illustration of the storms that may in this life descend on the Church of God or on the individual believer. Our sky may, like Job, be calm and without cloud; then it happens. We find ourselves surrounded and distressed by many trials and anxieties. Our world collapses. We can envisage the Psalmist in his younger days when he rested by the still waters, in those solitudes where, as a shepherd boy, he sang the immortal words,

> *The Lord's my Shepherd, I'll not want;*
> *He makes me down to lie*
> *In pastures green: He leadeth me*
> *The quiet waters by.*

Then came those storms which distressed his life over the years. But his latter end was peace. And what storms descend on the Church of God in this world! 'In this world ye shall have tribulation.' There are days of great tribulation still to come. 'In the last days perilous times shall come.' But – 'The Lord sitteth upon the flood.' He reigns as our King for ever. In the Gospel we read of how Christ by one brief word stilled the storm which terrified His disciples. 'Peace, be still.' 'And there was a great calm.' The awful storm which made the heart of the prophet to quake was followed

[57]

by 'a still small voice' which brought unspeakable peace to his spirit.

God's promise to His people is – 'O, thou afflicted, tossed with tempest and not comforted, behold, I will lay thy stones with fair colours, and lay thy foundations with sapphires . . . thou shalt be far from oppression; for thou shalt not fear: and from terror, for it shall not come near thee.' The world which God's people shall inhabit when they leave this world is one of everlasting peace.

A Christian minister once visited a hospital where he saw a dying young woman whose face radiated peace. With much tenderness and solemnity she repeated the famous stanza:

> *In peace let me resign my breath,*
> *And thy salvation see,*
> *My sins deserve eternal death,*
> *But Jesus died for me.*

## PSALM 30: THE SAINTS JUSTIFY GOD
### 'At the remembrance of his holiness'

David was once guilty of a great indiscretion. Contrary to God's will, he would number the people. The Divine rebuke was immediate. God gave him his choice of three forms of punishment. 'Let me,' he said, 'now fall into the hand of the Lord, for his mercies are great: and let me not fall into the hand of man.' And for three days the Lord's hand was heavy on the nation. With

God, however, David found no fault, but only with himself. To him God's visitation was a display of His justice and holiness – 'I know, O Lord, that thy judgments are right, and that thou in faithfulness hast afflicted me.'

In days of prosperity and comfort it may be difficult to distinguish between true godliness and its mere form. Often it is in the day of testing that the mask comes off and our real selves are discovered. Job's spouse would have him curse God in his day of adversity. But this he could not do, for God's grace was in his heart. 'Though he slay me, yet will I trust in him.' 'Love suffereth long.' The true believer would rather suffer than find fault with God in what He allows.

Once I stood at the bedside of a woman in hospital. Over the years she had been a church-going person, and her profession of religion seemed real enough. But, unlike the one I have mentioned in the previous Psalm, she had one great grievance in the hour of trial – 'What have I done that this should happen to me?' Only the saints can praise God at the remembrance of His holiness and when, for their sins, they come under His loving rebuke. They also know that it is along the path of affliction that they come to the place 'where the inhabitant shall not say, I am sick'.

'Thou shalt hide them'

The Psalmist's life was truly a miracle of preservation. There were hours when, to use his own words, he felt that there was but one step between him and death. The people of God in every age have had the same awareness of being exposed to constant danger; but their 'life is hid with Christ in God'. 'The name of the Lord is a strong tower; the righteous runneth into it, and is safe.' How real was this to David when, in the name of the God of Israel, and with no armour of mail to protect him, he faced the giant of Gath and the army of the Philistines! God was his invisible shield. God's presence with His people is something at which the forces of darkness tremble. He is to them as a pillar of fire by night and as a pillar of cloud by day. There are many lovely figures used of God in His Word which describe the safety of His 'hidden ones'. He carries them in His bosom. They are in the clefts of the Rock of Ages beyond the reach of those who seek their hurt. They are the apple of His eye. They are in the hollow of His hand. They are under His wings. He is their strong tower; their pavilion and their eternal home. Into His hands they commit their lives, their times and all their cares. In the highest sense no one knows where God's 'hidden ones' are but He Himself alone. Is not this the meaning of the words which He uses with regard to His people both in this Psalm and in the Song of Solomon? They are in 'the secret of his presence', and 'in the *secret places* of the stairs'. Therefore, let our song and prayer be that of another:

## Psalm 32

*Hide me, O my Saviour, hide,*
*Till the storm of life is past;*
*Safe into the haven guide;*
*O receive my soul at last.*

### PSALM 32: 'THE LORD OUR RIGHTEOUSNESS'

'Blessed is the man to whom the Lord imputeth not iniquity'

In these words the Psalmist touches on the great doctrine of imputation. This is the theme which Paul expounds in the Epistle to the Romans. It is a doctrine which is fundamental to our acceptance with God. Christ stands in a federal, or covenant, relationship to all His people. The guilt of Adam's first transgression belongs to us as well as to himself. He was the federal head of all mankind, and when he fell, all mankind became involved in his tragedy and guilt. But all the sins of God's people were imputed to Christ. Voluntarily, and in love, He took our sins upon Himself. His death was, therefore, vicarious and substitutionary. 'He was wounded for our transgressions; he was bruised for our iniquities.' In His unblemished life He honoured God's law which was broken at our hands. In His death He endured its penalty, which was death. And He arose again for our justification. Our exoneration from the penalty of sin, and our justification at the bar of God's justice, come through faith in His name as 'the Lord our righteousness'. When by faith we embrace Him, His righteousness becomes ours as if it were our own. We are 'accepted in the Beloved'. Through His

merits our transgression is forgiven and for ever erased
out of God's sight. The handwriting of ordinances which
was against us, He nailed to His cross.

A Christian lady – the Duchess of Gordon – retired to
bed one night with her sins looming before her like
great mountains. When at last sleep touched her eyes,
God visited her soul. A luminous scroll on which the
words, 'The Lord our righteousness' were inscribed,
began to unfold itself before her eyes. Then she awoke
to rejoice in Him who had clothed her soul in His own
best robe.

> *Not now by words bringing death to transgressors,*
> *Grace unto life the new covenant brings,*
> *Jesus our Surety, our Kinsman-Redeemer,*
> *Round us the robe of His righteousness flings.*

'O the happiness' [such is the original Hebrew] of
all who are in such a state! 'I will greatly rejoice in the
Lord; my soul shall be joyful in my God, for he hath
clothed me with the garments of salvation; he hath
covered me with the robe of righteousness.' Once I
sat in a pulpit and listened to an old friend who preached
a remarkable sermon on this theme. I still remember
his words: 'He who prepared this robe is he who
puts it on His people. Yes, and He will never never
take it off them.' 'The King's daughter is all glorious
within: her clothing is of wrought gold.' It is the glorious
and finished work of Christ.

God's people have been brought into a new world, the spiritual climate of which is the reverse of the old. 'For lo, the winter is past, the rain is over and gone; the flowers appear on the earth; the time of the singing of birds is come; and the voice of the turtle is heard in our land.' Emmanuel's land, into which Christ calls His people, is a place of songs. Those who inhabit it are aware of their indebtedness to God. When Israel got safely through the Red Sea, they sang for joy: 'I will sing unto the Lord, for he hath triumphed gloriously: the horse and his rider hath he thrown into the sea. The Lord is my strength and song, and he is become my salvation.' When David brought the ark of the Lord back to Zion, 'he danced before the Lord with all his might'. All the people brought God's ark to its resting place with songs. It was in truth the hour of David's greatest joy in this world.

Our sweetest song has its source in the sorrows and sufferings of the Redeemer. His own holy lips engaged in praise before He went to the Cross. 'And when they had sung an hymn they went out into the Mount of Olives.' This song was the earnest of that unending song of the great multitude who shall for ever stand in His presence. It was a song which preceded the praise of His followers when, after His ascension to Heaven, 'they returned to Jerusalem with great joy, and were continually in the temple praising and blessing God'. He had gone to prepare a place for them, and soon they would see Him again. They rejoiced in their great privilege in serving their Lord, and in suffering for Him.

When, for example, Paul and Silas were cast into

the inner prison, 'they sang praises unto God; and the prisoners heard them'. 'Blessed are ye when men shall revile you and persecute you ... Rejoice and be exceeding glad, for great is your reward in heaven.'

Is there anything in this world more like heaven than the praises of the Church of Christ when her heart is moved by His love? In the Scottish Highlands during the great evangelical revival as many as eight thousand people would gather together at communion seasons. To many present, such occasions brought them into the very vestibule of heaven. Often they sang these words:

> *The praises of thy wonders, Lord,*
> *The heavens shall express;*
> *And in the congregation*
> *Of saints thy faithfulness.*

'Praise *waiteth* for thee, O God, in Sion.'

PSALM 34: 'O TASTE AND SEE'

David was a poet without a compeer in history. His great gift God used to His own glory and to the good of His people to the end of time. The Spirit of the Lord spoke by him. His holy songs express the believer's trials, joys and hopes in a way no one else has ever done, or ever shall.

But there was one aspect of the Christian life which David was unable fully to express in words or convey to others. It was the enjoyment of communion with God. 'O taste and see that the Lord is good.' The order in which these words is put is significant. We 'taste' and then 'see'. Illumination comes through participation. It is when God communicates Himself to the soul that we discover the unspeakable wonder of such a favour. When Jonathan tasted of the honey which lay about him on the ground his eyes were opened. Light came with the life. So it is in Christian experience. 'In him was life, and the life was the light of men.'

God communicates Himself to the soul through the written Word. 'His mouth,' said the Church, 'is most sweet.' 'How sweet are thy words unto my taste! Yea, sweeter than honey to my mouth!' He does it also through prayer. In verse 6 of our Psalm David speaks of himself as the poor man who cries to God. God hears his prayer and saves him out of all his troubles. How unspeakably precious is the throne of grace when God imparts the blessing of His presence to the soul! 'I sat down under His shadow with great delight and His fruit was sweet to my taste.' A preacher once used an illustration appropriate to our theme. He spoke of one who sat under a tall tree laden with wholesome, ripe fruit, but its branches were beyond her reach. She would fain have tasted of the fruit but could not. Then it happened! A strong, warm gust of wind wafted through its branches giving her a lapful of the desired fruit. The Holy Spirit is like the wind that 'bloweth where it listeth'. When He gives us a measure of spiritual quickening, at the same time He refreshes our needy souls with the fruit of the Tree of Life. Then we say, 'O taste and see that the Lord is good!' In this way

God sustains His people. 'Stay me with flagons, comfort me with apples, for I am sick with love.'

Often have I told the story of the missionary who once met a native boy in the way. The missionary carried a bag of sweets. He gave some to the lad and told him to put one in his mouth. He had never tasted anything like it before. With a look of astonishment in his eyes he ran toward his native heath and began to tell his friends about what he had under his tongue. They plied him with questions – 'What is it like?' 'How does it taste?' His answer was, 'Here, try it for yourselves, and then you will know'. We may argue about God, His existence, and the external evidences which the universe and providence provide. But only when His love and presence touch our hearts can we really know Him in His unspeakable goodness.

A man once told an anecdote of two small boys whose mother gave them a small portion of honey from a big dish which she wisely kept out of their reach. After they had eaten, the one said to the other: 'This is good, but it will be far better when the big dish up above is set before us.' The man remarked: 'God's people enjoy a taste of God here; but the day is coming when by "the brooks of honey" in the heavenly Canaan their souls shall be for ever satisfied with His abundant goodness.'

> *How great's the goodness thou for them*
> *That fear thee keep'st in store,*
> *And wrought'st for them that trust in thee*
> *The sons of men before!*

The origin of evil is a great mystery. In the words of a famous divine, Did Satan take his eye off the God whom he was created to glorify and adore? Did he turn his eye upon himself as one who should be also worshipped? That pride was the first sin of those angels who kept not their first estate comes to light in Satan's first approach to man – 'Ye shall be as gods'. This was the dark abyss which engulfed those evil spirits and which brought man so low. Man's persistent misery and folly may be traced to his pride, the evil root which Satan embedded in his soul. History is a portrayal of man's pride. Men and races departed from God only to be reduced to ignominy and bitter woe. Where is Herod? Where is Nebuchadnezzar? Where are Alexander the Great, Adolf Hitler, and countless others who sought their own glory and not God's?

Our true happiness begins when we turn our eyes from ourselves and from man and see no one 'save Jesus only'. A person once spoke about the process of self-elimination through which he passed before he could say with John the Baptist, 'He must increase, but I must decrease'. It began with 'Christ and I'. It ended with 'Jesus only' or 'the Lord be magnified'. How proud was Paul as on the day of his conversion he approached Damascus! But he was soon in the dust of self-abasement. And there he remained to the end. With only a step between him and heaven he was still, in his own estimation, the chief of sinners. O how great a gulf lay between him and the so-called successors of the apostles who, under proud names, sit on papal thrones and lordly benches! Only that grace which enables us to see ourselves as we are, and which opens our eyes to behold the infinite majesty of God, can produce this ever-deepening desire in our souls – 'The Lord be magnified'.

Once, as I walked along a street in one of our Scottish cities, I saw a poor plainly dressed woman who carried a placard on which these very words were inscribed, 'The Lord be magnified'. On that day trumpets blared, men bowed the one to the other as they passed into a large, well-known church. In contrast to all such displays are the words – 'To this man will I look, even to him that is poor and of a contrite spirit and trembleth at my word'.

## PSALM 36: THE BOW IN THE CLOUD
### 'His faithfulness reacheth unto the clouds'

These words, we believe, are related to God's covenant promise to Noah when, after many days on the bosom of the flood, he emerged safely from the ark. God's righteous judgment had been exercised in the destruction of the evil world; but now man and all the creatures whom God had preserved, were embraced within a covenant promise that such a deluge of water would never again destroy the earth. 'O Lord, thou preservest man and beast.' As the symbol of His covenant faithfulness, God set His bow in the clouds.

But Noah, as a child of that covenant 'which is ordered in all things and sure', could see in that lovely symbol not only the promise of his physical preservation, but also the guarantee of his eternal security in Christ

who is the Prince of Peace. God's covenant with the
creature is within the context of time, but His covenant
with His people extends to the eternal world. 'For this
is as the waters of Noah unto me; for as I have sworn
that the waters of Noah should no more go over the
earth, so have I sworn that I would not be wroth with
thee, nor rebuke thee. For the mountains shall depart
and the hills be removed, but my kindness shall not
depart from thee, neither shall the covenant of my
peace be removed, saith the Lord that hath mercy on
thee.'

'Great shall be the peace of thy children.' In that
lovely upper world, where no tempest shall ever assail
the church of God, there is a rainbow, like unto an
emerald, round about the throne on which our Lord
sits. Tempests are approaching our world; but 'the
Lord on high is mightier than the noise of many waters'.
His bow will remain in the cloud here, and when the
clouds of time pass away it will still adorn the throne
of God above.

### PSALM 37: OUR ORDERED FOOTSTEPS
'The steps of a good man are ordered by the Lord'

To the people of God there is no such thing as 'luck'
nor are any happenings merely 'accidental'. However
sudden, unexpected, or even dramatic, some events in
our life may be, all are ordered by the divine mind.
Were all the events of our life, small and great, ordered
the moment we were born, or when we reached the

years of maturity or responsibility? No! From all
eternity God has foreordained whatsoever comes to
pass. All the events of our life here were known to and
arranged by an all-wise and omniscient God.

We have in the Bible many examples of how God
orders the steps of His saints. God's directing voice
reached the ear of Abraham when He told him to
leave his place and people and to go to a land which
he and his seed were afterwards to receive for an
inheritance. The glorious destiny which God had
decreed for him was, step by step, unveiled before his
eyes. It was God who led Moses into the place where
He committed to his charge the task of leading His
people out of Egypt into the land of promise. Who led
the woman to the well of Sychar at the very moment
when her Redeemer appeared on the scene? In his
epistles Paul speaks of the way in which God, by His
word and providence, led him into those places where
the Gospel must be preached, and into the path of men
and women who were to inherit His kingdom. God's
people are guided in all their ways by His Word – 'This
is the way, walk ye in it.'

While God's way is safe it is not always an easy
way. It often leads through the 'vale of tears'. Men like
Jacob, Job, Asaph, David and Daniel were led to their
eternal rest along the way of frowning providences and
great trials; but 'he knoweth the way that I take, and
when he hath tried me I shall come forth as gold'.
In this way we may often feel discouraged but, 'Though
he fall he shall not be utterly cast down, for the Lord
upholdeth him with his hand'. The Psalm tells us that
He who leads his child step by step, 'delighteth in his

way'. He delights in those who remain in the way of obedience. When, like Jonah, we would go our own way, we come under His rebuke, so that we may be led again into the way of obedience.

Life in retrospect is the proof of God's wise ordering of our steps. Where had we been if He had not kept us, and guided us? Only in heaven shall we fully know His wisdom, and how constant was His care of us here. 'In that day ye shall ask me nothing.'

Philip Doddridge, the famous divine, used to tell of a time when he was suddenly stricken down by the Lord's hand. He could not understand why the Lord thus dealt with him at a time when he was so actively engaged in His work. One night he went to bed and dreamed. In his dream he found himself in heaven and within the mansion which the Lord – who was present there – had prepared for him. In the room where he stood he was amazed to see written on the wall before his eyes all the events of his life. They were all explained, including his present state of disablement. He awoke greatly reassured that all his footsteps were ordered by the Lord, both to His own glory and to his own everlasting good.

## PSALM 38: 'THE LOATHSOME DISEASE'

God pronounces the heart of man to be 'desperately wicked' and beyond all human understanding. The external world with all its lawlessness and evils is but a mild reflection of man's heart.

Every true child of God makes a measure of discovery of his native sinfulness. This is because God's Spirit enters his soul with God's Word, which is both a lamp and a sword. The lamp throws its beam of light upon his darkened, sinful soul, while the sword cuts through all the veneer and deception by which his sin is concealed. A dead man has no awareness of his own corruption; and the soul which is dead in trespasses and sins has no true consciousness of the evil within.

Even in a state of grace 'the plague of the heart' is what increasingly distresses the believer. It gives him pain. The more he grows in holiness, the more he cries with Paul and Isaiah, 'In me, that is, in my flesh, there dwelleth no good thing'. 'Woe is me, for I am a man of unclean lips.' Spiritual pain is a necessary part of our sanctification. God's love often knocks at our door in the garments of pain.

Two things remain with those who know this plague. The one is prayer; the other is desire. 'Heal my soul, for I have sinned against thee.' For all who have this prayer, there is balm in Gilead and there is a physician there.

'Lord, all my desire is before thee.' What was his desire? That the day would come when he would be for ever separated from, and purged of, this plague. And God will fulfil the desire of all who fear Him. 'Who healeth all thy diseases.' Every prayer and desire which the Spirit of God has generated in our soul, God will hear and fulfil. The hearer of prayer is the One who also says – 'I am the Lord who healeth thee'.

'While I was musing the fire burned'

A good man once found himself walking along a quiet, country road in the Highlands of Scotland. There was nothing around him to disturb his peace. 'What a lovely place for meditation,' he whispered to himself. Meditation, prayer and praise should go together. The excellent Thomas Watson once remarked that meditation and prayer are like two turtle-doves. If we separate them, 'one dies and the other pines'.

Perhaps at this time of spiritual depression the Psalmist was recalling other and kinder days. Sometimes when we read our Bibles we recall other days. We remember sermons and seasons of sweet communion with the Lord and His people. We recall our seasons of secret enjoyments when we could say – 'My Beloved is mine, and I am his'.

There is an Emmaus walk, we believe, in the life-history of many believers. We sometimes walk in the way and are sad. We begin to muse on the sufferings and glory of Him who is the Rose of Sharon and the Lily of the valleys. Then, suddenly, our meditation of Him is sweetened by His presence. 'Did not our hearts burn within us while He talked with us by the way, and while He opened to us the Scriptures?' The great Pascal could never forget the night when, alone in his room, and meditating on spiritual things, he suddenly became aware of God's presence. The love and the awe of the eternal 'I AM' possessed his spirit. All he could say was – 'Fire, fire, fire! The God of Abraham, the God of Isaac and the God of Jacob.' At that moment he discovered that God was the all in all, and that, by His sovereign grace, he was a spiritual contemporary of all the saints and in the embrace of that God to whom all time is as 'a watch in the night'.

In the Song of Solomon the mystical Bride, thinking of her Lord, was moved in her soul when the Beloved put in His hand through the hole of the door. She just saw His hand. How did she know that it was His hand? And why did a sight of His hand so deeply move her heart in love to Him? That hand bore the prints of the nails, the eternal proof of His love to her. There, like the one whom we mentioned before, she saw her own name engraven; this made her leave her bed to seek Him. The holy flame of His love was kindled anew in her soul, the fire which the floods cannot drown.

### PSALM 40: 'YE ARE MY WITNESSES'

'I have declared thy faithfulness ... I have not concealed thy lovingkindness'

An impressive characteristic of some of the Messianic Psalms is the way in which they lend themselves to a twofold interpretation. In a minor and subordinate manner, the sufferings and the witness of the Church, or the believer, have their reflection in the witness and sufferings of Christ. Here we have the blessed Redeemer prophetically making His appeal to God the Father that He had given the world a perfect and final revelation of His love and His faithfulness. He held nothing back.

The three thoughts which confront us in this passage are: the great messenger; the great congregation; and the great theme. Christ is the supreme Messenger and Prophet of His Church. The prophet Isaiah anticipated His coming into this world when he wrote: 'How beautiful upon the mountains are the feet of him that bringeth good tidings, that publisheth peace; that bringeth good tidings of good, that publisheth salvation; that saith unto Zion, thy God reigneth.' And when He did appear on the scene of time, His words were: 'The Spirit of the Lord God is upon me, because the Lord hath anointed me to preach good tidings unto the meek.' Those who listened to His words confessed, 'Never man spake like this man'. He had the tongue of the learned.

The 'great congregation' to whom our Lord declared God's lovingkindness embraces the whole world: 'Look unto me, and be ye saved, all the ends of the earth; for I am God and there is none else.' 'Beside me there is no Saviour.' When He finished His work, He gave a command to His apostles: 'Go ye into all the world and preach the Gospel to every creature.'

And what is the great theme of the Gospel? The greatest words ever uttered, or that ever shall be uttered, in this world, fell from His lips in His conversation with Nicodemus: 'For God so loved the world that he gave his only begotten Son, that whosoever believeth in him should not perish but have everlasting life.'

Now the Lord's people who know the love of Christ, and to whom He is precious in every conceivable way, all have a story to tell. A sincere and simple-minded man whom the Lord had rescued from a godless life would sometimes say to his fellow-sinners, 'He saved me, and He will never hear the end of it'. When that love, which is 'better than wine', is shed abroad in our hearts we, like the apostles, cannot but speak of the things which we have seen and heard.

A man once gave his witness at a public meeting. He told the story of a number of men who, in the old days, found a cask of wine on an island shore. They opened the cask and refreshed themselves with a small measure of its contents. After hiding it in a remote corner they agreed to keep the matter a secret. But when, later on in the day, they came to their native village, 'the refreshment' which had warmed their hearts had also unloosed their tongues. So they told their neighbours about their find. The good man then said that those who had tasted that the Lord is gracious cannot always conceal what is in their hearts. Dr John Kennedy, of Dingwall, who was present at the service, commended the illustration as appropriate in its higher and spiritual application. If Christ the hope of glory and His love are in our hearts we, like His followers on the Day of Pentecost, cannot conceal it. 'He could not be hid.' We are made vessels unto honour, to *show forth* the praises of Him who hath called us out of darkness into His marvellous light. Have we also a story to tell? Did the Lord put a new song in our mouth because He put His own love in our heart?

'By this I know that thou favourest me, because mine
enemy doth not triumph over me'

There are many who lie on the lap of a great deception.
They believe that their temporal comforts, and the
absence of much trouble within the sphere of providence,
are a proof of God's love to them. But as we know in
the light of Scripture, the reverse is often, if not always,
the case. In another Psalm Asaph speaks of the wicked
as moving toward destruction on a calm sea while the
righteous had 'a full cup' of affliction meted out to
them. Esau was rejected of God; but He gave him the
quiet, pastoral and fertile land of Mount Seir while
'Joseph and his brethren went down to Egypt'. He
knew nothing of 'the afflictions of Joseph'.

Many reasons could be mentioned why the Lord
allows these conflicts to enter our lives. One is that we
may know, in a measure, the great dangers from which
He saves us. All true Christians discover sooner or later
that Satan is bent on their destruction. But those whom
God loves shall be kept by His power. A famous preacher
once wrote: 'What a wonder it is that when the devil
enters the lists with a poor, erring, bedridden, deserted,
slandered saint, . . . he cannot win the day, but in the
end slinks off without renown.'

*The feeblest saint shall win the day,*
*Though death and hell obstruct his way.*

It is in our sorrow that we discover how great is His
love. Think, for example, of the home in Bethany
where the Lord sometimes tarried, and where by His
words and presence He rejoiced the hearts of His loved
ones. Then it happened. A cloud of sorrow descended

on that favoured home. Lazarus was stricken down. And the loved Lord was far removed from them in the hour of grief. Their urgent plea that He might come to their help He did not answer immediately. Then death did its work, and not until the one 'whom the Lord loved' had lain in the grave for four days did He arrive on the scene.

Was He indifferent? Ah, no! It was in that hour that He manifested His infinite power over death and the grave. It was in that hour that the depths of love and sympathy within His being surfaced in the presence of men. 'Jesus wept.' 'Behold how he loved him!' It was this event which also brought from His lips words which bring unspeakable comfort to all His people. 'I am the resurrection and the life: he that believeth in me, though he were dead, yet shall he live: and whoso-ever liveth and believeth in me shall never die.' The home of tears became again the place of consolation. They knew that day, as they never did before, that they were in the presence of One who would one day bring them, beyond the reach of death and the grave, into the place where these are unknown.

### PSALM 42: MEMORIES OF OTHER DAYS

'I will remember thee from the land of Jordan, and of the Hermonites, from the hill Mizar'

Often when we think of other days our hearts are deeply moved. We think of dear friends in the Lord who are no longer here. We recall seasons of spiritual enjoyment when 'with the multitude' we went to God's house. It was so with the Psalmist. We are not to conclude, however, that his days of loneliness and isolation were without many gleams of comfort and many hours of communion with God.

Would it be presumptuous to say that the three places named in the verse are typical of certain Christian experiences? There is 'the land of Jordan', 'the Hermonites' and 'the hill Mizar'. We cannot tell what memories David associated with these places but, like him, each believer has his own cherished memories of other days and places.

Historically, 'the land of Jordan' is the place where Israel, on their long journey to the Promised Land, were confronted with the dark stream which they could not cross, but God divided the waters and the people went over without fear. God's people on their way to heaven are often confronted with fears and problems. With Jacob, however, and figuratively they can say, 'With my rod and my staff have I crossed over this Jordan'. He whose 'way is in the sea and his path in the great waters', knows how to make a way of escape for His people out of all their fears and temptations.

There are seasons in our life which, however, are the reverse of these; times when we are transported in our souls to that mount on which the dew of heaven rests, and where we say, 'Lord, it is good for us to be here'. Jacob had his Bethel hour. Moses could ever remember the day when 'the good will of him that dwelt in the bush' brought a foretaste of heaven into his soul. Paul had his season of joy in the third heaven.

A godly minister in Canada – the Rev John Anderson of Glengarry – used to speak of 'a stone of remembrance' or of a place 'where alone with God he often enjoyed communion with Him'.

Once, as I stood at the bedside of a gracious and elderly lady, she spoke to me of 'a day of heaven on earth' when, after a communion service, she was afraid that even her contact with her Christian friends would disturb her deep peace and her sense of God's presence. She would rather be alone. The language of her heart was that of the bride in the Song: 'I charge you that ye stir not up nor awake my love till He please.'

It was of Mount Hermon that David said in another psalm that 'there the Lord commanded the blessing, even life for evermore'. But God's people are not always, or often, in such a state of spiritual elevation. How thankful we should be that 'the little hills' may bring us peace as well as 'the lofty mountains'! The word 'Mizar' means 'a little hill' which anyone, however feeble, might climb. The Apostle Peter, who was with Christ on the Mount of Transfiguration, subordinated that great event and enjoyment to the faith of God's people in His Word. Listen to his words: 'For he received from God the Father honour and glory, when there came such a voice to him from the excellent glory, This is my beloved Son in whom I am well pleased. And this voice which came from heaven we heard when we were with him in the holy mount. We have also a more sure word of prophecy, whereunto ye do well that ye take heed, as unto a light that shineth in a dark place, until the day dawn and the day star arise in your hearts.' It was Margaret MacDiarmaid, known in her day as 'the woman of great faith', who referred to herself as 'the woman of little faith in a great God'. And is not our 'little faith in a great God' a sure proof that we are in the footsteps of the flock?

PSALM 43: THE SIN OF SELF-PITY

'Why art thou cast down, O my soul'

Self-pity was something which sought to invade the soul of David in the midst of his many sorrows. He addresses his own soul with a series of questions. Why this groundless fear and agitation? Why these persistent doubts and anxieties? There is in the Psalm a recognition that self-pity is dishonouring to God. It often springs from unbelief.

There are innumerable reasons why we should not harbour this attitude to ourselves. One of them is the relation in which God stands to us as His children. He is our Father in Heaven. And those who have discovered the compassion which is in His heart toward them should never pity themselves. It was in love and in pity that He redeemed us:

> *Such pity as a father hath*
> *Unto his children dear,*
> *Like pity shows the Lord to such*
> *As worship him in fear.*

The pity which is in the heart of a mother toward her ailing child has no equal in the world of nature, but the Lord reminds us that even a mother's care may break down, but His is never-failing. 'Can a woman forget her sucking child, that she should not have compassion on the son of her womb? yea, they may forget, yet will I not forget thee.' Those whom God pities, and who are to enjoy everlasting fellowship with Him, should never pity themselves.

As the shadow of dejection touched David's mind, the grace of hope, like a ray of light, shot through it and dispelled the gloom. 'Hope thou in God.' As Paul reminds us, hope is the anchor of the soul.

> *We have an anchor that keeps the soul*
> *Steadfast and sure while the billows roll:*
> *Fastened to the rock which cannot move,*
> *Grounded firm and deep in the Saviour's love.*

Let us reflect for a moment on the One in whom we hope. It is He who has all power in heaven and on earth, and out of whose hand none of His people shall ever be plucked. In His hand we are as safe – though not as happy – as those who are already in Heaven.

David anticipates his eventual deliverance from all his trials when he speaks of God as 'the health of his countenance'. Sometimes when we stand before the mirror we may see signs of age, infirmity and ill-health in our face. But the day is coming when He shall present us to Himself 'not having spot or wrinkle or any such thing'. 'They shall see his face and *his name* shall be in their foreheads.'

'Awake, why sleepest thou, O Lord?'

God never sleeps. Sleep, as such, is one of His precious and restorative gifts to His creatures. The words of this prayer mean that God may sometimes remain silent to the cry of His people. He may seem to them to tarry long with His response. He may, in the midst of their helplessness, give no immediate manifestation of His power in coming to their help. While this apparent silence is one of the griefs of His people, a godless world may, at the same time, ridicule their faith – 'Where is thy God?' 'Is there any knowledge in the most High?'

But God's ear is ever open to the cry of His people. He will awake. When this happens He exercises His power in a twofold manner. He brings the ungodly under the rod of His indignation. 'Then the Lord awaked as one out of sleep, and like a mighty man that shouteth by reason of wine, and he smote his enemies and put them to a perpetual reproach.' He can be terrible to the kings of the earth and to all who touch the apple of His eye. This is the solemn lesson of history.

> Avenge, O Lord, thy slaughtered saints, whose bones
>   Lie scattered on the Alpine mountains cold . . .
> Forget not: in thy book record their groans
>   Who were thy sheep.

God can in the same hour 'command deliverances for Jacob', and stretch the rod of His strength out of Zion. It was in the hour of his greatest fear that Moses, at the command of God, addressed Israel in these words: 'Stand still and see the salvation of the Lord.'

A little while ago I had a visit from a friend. We discussed the display of God's power seen in the recent defeat and humiliation of the enemies of Israel [1967]. My friend remarked that it was an event more awe-inspiring in its suddenness and irresistible power than the destruction of Pharaoh and his hosts in the Red Sea. It was, we believe, one of the preludes of the glad day when, through the outpouring of the Holy Spirit, the seed of Abraham shall emerge out of their spiritual grave to recognize their glorious Messiah.

Meantime let us pray: 'Awake, awake, put on strength, O arm of the Lord; awake, as in the ancient days, in the generations of old.' 'Awake, O north wind, and come, thou south; blow upon my garden, . . . Let my beloved come into his garden.' In these words we see the Church of God on her knees and praying for the promised day of His power.

When Christ was asleep in the ship, it was not the sound of the storm that awoke Him out of His sleep, but the cry or the prayers of His disciples. May He give us the grace to wrestle with Him and, like Jacob at Peniel, may we refuse to let Him go till He gives us His blessing.

'Men ought always to pray and not to faint.'

'Instead of thy fathers shall be thy children whom tho mayest make princes in all the earth'

The Lord shall have His witnesses in the world 'as long as the sun and moon endure, throughout all generations'. How wonderfully this is brought before us in that glorious genealogical chain written in the Gospel! It begins with Adam and ends with the arrival of Christ, 'the bright and morning Star'. If the old dispensation ended with His coming, a new and a better era began in the very hour when He finished His work in righteousness. He will, indeed, have His witnesses in this world to the end of time.

It is a characteristic of all the heirs of salvation that they pray for the children whom God promises and gives them. The lovely story of Hannah who, through her earnest prayer, was given the promise that God would bless her with a man child, tells us also of her resolve to give back to the Lord the precious gift He had lent her. And through her child God preserved a pure witness in the nation while he lived.

Thousands of years afterwards, in one of our Scottish parishes, a gracious woman was similarly blessed with 'a son of promise'. Because she believed that he would live to proclaim the unsearchable riches of Christ, she named him Samuel. And so it was. Her son became a sincere minister of Christ. He passed to his rest and reward after faithfully serving his generation in the Gospel. This was the well-beloved Samuel MacIver, minister in Kilmuir Easter in Ross-shire.

There was a man who once retired to pray. As he stood before the Lord the thought impressed itself upon his mind that he should pray that as God had preserved a true witness in the family to which he belonged for several generations, He might continue this great favour in the generations to come. And one morning these very words deeply touched his spirit: 'Instead of thy fathers shall be thy children.' There and then he bowed his knee in thanksgiving to God.

It was through his prayer that Jacob was given the name 'a prince with God'. By the standards of this poor and passing world such men are not recognized as 'princes', but often as the 'off-scourings of the world'. Only in the higher dimension of grace are they God's princes in the earth.

One day, in the city of Glasgow, I called on a good woman. News had just reached us that a faithful servant of Christ had been taken Home. In a low, broken voice she repeated the words, 'Know ye not that there is a prince and a great man fallen this day in Israel?'

These princes of God often go with the good news to the remote and dark places of the earth. The history of the Christian Church is replete with such bright stars, with the records of men who went forth with 'good news from a far country'. And if there are times when the Church of Christ is, spiritually speaking, like a barren woman, His promise to her remains, 'Thy sons shall come from far, and thy daughters shall be nursed at thy side'.

> *The barren woman house to keep*
> *He maketh, and to be*
> *Of sons a mother full of joy.*
> *Praise to the Lord give ye.*

### 'Be still, and know that I am God'

These solemn words may be given a twofold application. They are addressed both to a godless world, and also to the Church of God. In the heathen, pagan world around us, many and loud are the voices which may be heard. There are those who deny God's existence, or who 'could not care less', and there are those who make a god in their own image. There are those who, when they speak in opposition to God, think they can 'get away with it'. 'Thou thoughtest that I was altogether such an one as thyself; but I will reprove thee, and set them [thine iniquities] in order before thine eyes.' Many in our age, under the name of 'Christian' speak of God as tolerant, even of evil. He will punish no one, for all are His children. But God is holy; God is just. He will in no wise clear the guilty who remain unrepentant in their sins. His wrath is revealed from Heaven against all ungodliness and unrighteousness of men. For the sins of this age we fear that He is soon going to speak to us in judgment. Then all hostile voices will be silenced. 'The earth feared and was still when God arose in judgment, to save all the meek of the earth.'

The words speak also to those of God's people who may be passing through many adversities. Let me illustrate. In the town of Stornoway, with the dawn of the year 1919, a minister of Christ was in his study preparing a sermon. An island of twenty-seven thousand inhabitants had, in one hour, become a place of weeping. The night before, over two hundred men perished within sight of their native shore. The Great War was over. Mothers, fathers, wives, sweethearts and sisters were waiting to welcome home their loved ones, who had passed through years of stress and storm. But there they perished within sight of their homes. The church that day was full. All heads were bowed and tears dropped from many eyes. The minister gave out his text – 'Be still, and know that I am God'. A stillness did pervade the island for many days. The very waves which spent themselves on its shores seemed to echo the words, 'Be still, and know that I am God'.

These words, however, are for many of God's people, full of comfort. Let me again illustrate. A man who was in the grip of spiritual depression was reading a book. In the past God had been kind to him in applying to his soul many great and precious promises. Now he was afraid that the promises which so often had been his comfort could not belong to such a sinner as he felt himself to be. Then, as he read the book, these words of one of the Puritan divines met his eyes: ' "Be still and know that I am God"; as if God had said: "Know ye, O ye wicked, that I am God, who can avenge myself when I please upon you; and cease to provoke me by your sins; *and know, ye trembling souls, that I am God, and therefore able to pardon the greatest sins, and cease to dishonour me by your unbelieving thoughts of me.*" Let every child of God, therefore, still his fears, for God's love and promise are as changeless as Himself. 'Peace; be still; fear not; I will never leave thee, nor forsake thee.'

'Sing praises to God'

When the soul passes out of the dead winter and bondage
of sin to enjoy the new 'dayspring from on high', God
becomes the subject of its praise. 'I will praise thee, O
Lord. Though thou wast angry with me, thine anger
is turned away, and thou comfortedst me.' In the
Bible we have many impressive instances of what one
might call the spiritual ecstasy which comes through
personal experience of God's love and mercy.

This ecstasy is not an irrational emotion. It is the
expression of that joy which is 'unspeakable and full of
glory'. It is a joy that sometimes touches the hearts of
all believers. Let me give one or two examples of this.

A minister of Christ once preached a soul-refreshing
sermon in a certain church in the city of Glasgow.
Leading the praise was a choice young man who, like
many present, enjoyed through the message a great
blessing. As they sang the last Psalm this young man
turned to the minister in the pulpit behind him and
exclaimed in a joyous voice, 'You will be in glory, and
I will be in glory!' And they are together there now,
singing the praises of 'the Lamb in the midst of the
throne'. It was an incident which brought tears to
many eyes in the large congregation.

Once I sat by the bed of an old man who was led to
Christ in the evening of his days. In a subdued voice
he spoke of 'that wonderful morning' when God
transported his soul 'into the ocean of His love'. He
became, he said, oblivious to all things pertaining to
this lower world. God became his all and in all. Like
another, he wished for a thousand tongues to praise
his great Redeemer who had, in a love which passeth

# Psalm 48

knowledge, embraced him for ever. And I still seem to hear his voice softly repeating the word – 'wonderful, wonderful'.

As we look at this Psalm we observe that God's people praise and adore Him for what He is in His own essential Being. They praise Him for His love revealed in the gift and in the work of His dear Son, and for rescuing their souls from eternal death. 'Let Israel rejoice in him that made him; let the children of Zion be joyful in their King . . . Let the saints be joyful in glory.' They praise Him for those fuller enjoyments of His love awaiting them in the world to come. 'Praise waiteth for thee, O God, in Zion.'

## PSALM 48: OUR UNFADING INHERITANCE

'This God is our God for ever and ever; He will be our guide even unto death'

Dr John Kennedy of Dingwall once spoke on these words with great power and unction. The large congregation who listened to his words had a solemn awareness of God's presence among them. When his wife afterwards asked him to preach that sermon again, he declined. He felt that if he did, and if the same help and the same freedom were denied him, it would only damage his sweet recollection of the occasion when God so richly blessed His word to many of His people.

Although this Psalm was written within the dimension of time, and in the context of history, the God who is here spoken of as 'this God' is the ever-living I AM. 'Before Abraham was, I AM.'

There is in every one of us an instinctive fear of death, but united to Christ and in possession of everlasting life, we are for ever beyond the reach of death. These words could be translated correctly as, 'This God is our God from eternity to eternity. He will be our guide even unto death, over death and beyond death.' The shadow of death may pass over God's people when they come to cross the last river, but death itself cannot harm them. They dwell in God as their eternal home, into which death can never intrude.

O how endearing are these words – *'Our God, for ever and ever!'* He will also be our guide as we pass through each perplexing path of life. Equally endearing are the words, 'This God'. There is no place where He is not; but the place where He delights to dwell beyond all others is in the heart of His people, or in His own Zion. 'This is my rest for ever: here will I dwell; for I have desired it.' The people in whom and with whom He dwells He will bring at last to the place prepared for them above.

> *Thou, with thy counsel, while I live,*
> *Wilt me conduct and guide;*
> *And to thy glory afterward*
> *Receive me to abide.*

The story is told of an aged Christian minister who once listened to a friend who spoke to him about the amount of money and substance which a certain deceased person known to them both had left behind him. This old servant of God, who had but little of this world's goods, remarked that it was but little the deceased had left compared to what he himself would leave when he passed away. His friend, with evident surprise, said, 'I did not know that you had much to leave.' 'Yes,' said the minister, whose inheritance was above, 'when I die, I shall leave the whole world behind me.'

This Psalm is a perfect portrayal of man as he is 'having no hope, and without God in the world'. His roots are fixed in the things of this world, and in the precarious deception that life and the things which he possesses will go on just as they are. He envisages a long and prosperous future. Our Lord in the parable spoke of such an one. His barns were full. His health was good. He would now draw in his chair and 'enjoy life' and repose. Both he and those who depended on him would be secure 'for many years'. But within a few brief hours he was in the grip of death, with his soul wrapped up in eternal destitution and despair. And possibly, for the first time in his life this man was addressed as a 'fool', not by men, but by God.

How few learn the lesson that mere material things are remote and detached from our real selves. Man is essentially a soul, and the creation has absolutely nothing to satisfy him. The man who possessed more of this world's riches, pleasures and honour than any other, wrote 'emptiness and anxiety of spirit' over the whole. He discovered that for the soul of man the creation could not take the place of God. We leave the world either with God or nothing – apart from our sin and its dire consequences. John Bunyan gives us a picture of an earthbound man who went on day after day gathering straw with his muck-rake, his eyes glued to the earth. Above him was a crown of glory which he never saw. And if a man's eyes are set on things seen, he shall, in the words of the Psalm, 'never see light'.

This, then, should be our prayer: 'Open my eyes that I may see the wonders of thy Word. Open my heart that I may welcome Thee into my soul for ever.' The great and solemn question which confronts us all is, How shall I pass out of time – with God, or with nothing? Our deepest folly, and the greatest harm that we can inflict on our own beings, is to let God's goodness, and God Himself, pass us by unsought, despised and ignored.

### PSALM 50: THE FESTAL GATHERING

'Gather my saints together unto me: those that have made a covenant with me by sacrifice'

In these words God claims His people as His own. *My saints.* This means that they are all bought with a price, the blood of the everlasting covenant. Not only are they bought, but they are made to draw near to Him by that same blood of sprinkling. It is because He reconciles them to God by His death that Christ can pray: 'Father, I will that they also whom thou hast given me, be with me where I am.' 'And they shall be mine, saith the Lord of hosts, in that day when I make up my jewels.'

Their place of final rest is heaven. At death their souls immediately pass into glory, to be united again to their bodies at the resurrection. God speaks of the death of Abraham, and of all who have his faith, as a gathering of His people to Himself. 'And he was gathered to his people.' 'Absent from the body, present with the Lord.'

A few years ago a beloved friend wrote me, in quick succession, several letters expressing his fear that he was still a stranger to God. His heart was hard, and he felt that within him there was 'no good thing', only the thorns and briars of sin. He was aware that the day of grace was swiftly passing away. He spoke about his godly mother at whose knee he was often instructed in the ways of righteousness.

Personally I had no doubt that this man was a 'new creature' in Christ. Seldom did he listen to God's Word expounded from the pulpit but his eyes would fill. His deep affection for God's Word, God's house and people, was, to me, a proof that he had passed from death to life. There was an urgency and an earnestness about his letters which deeply touched me. Somehow I felt that, although he was still comparatively young and strong, he was nearing the end of life's journey.

Then one morning I suddenly awoke with God's Word on my lips. 'Gather my saints together unto me; those that have made a covenant with me by sacrifice.' I could not but believe that another of God's people had been taken Home. 'Who,' I asked myself, 'could it be?' Then the 'phone rang and a voice said: 'Did you notice in this morning's paper that Mr H—— is gone?' 'O,' I whispered to myself, 'what a sweet and lovely surprise my dear friend would get when, all of a sudden, he found himself in the realms of bliss, gathered to his people and to his God.'

There the great host of God's elect shall come to gather to their glorious Shiloh, for 'unto him shall the gathering of the people be'.

PSALM 51: THE SACRIFICE IN WHICH GOD DELIGHTS
'The sacrifices of God are a broken spirit'

The background of this Psalm is sad in the extreme. David had committed two sins for which the Mosaic law provided no forgiveness. For deliberate murder and adultery death was the inevitable penalty. He knew that before God there was no forgiveness through any sacrifices which he might offer or any gifts which he might present. With Micah he could have asked the solemn question: 'Will the Lord be pleased with thousands of rams or with ten thousands of rivers of oil? Shall I give my first-born for my transgression, the fruit of my body for the sin of my soul?' No! by such offerings God cannot be appeased. David might have said: 'If I build Him an house, a magnificent temple; if I plead my hitherto circumspect life and all my good deeds in His service, will these not compensate for my lapse, and restore me to His favour?' No! 'We are all

as an unclean thing, and all our righteousnesses are as
filthy rags.'

There is but one way back to God. And David knew
it. It is through the merits of the Lamb of God. His
first great plea, therefore, before God was, 'Purge me
with hyssop, and I shall be clean: wash me, and I shall
be whiter than snow.' He looked by faith to the One
who loved him and who was to give Himself for him.
As before God he pleaded for mercy, he, in an act of
faith, and like John Bunyan, bore the holy Child Jesus
in the arms of his soul. With his penitence and crushed
heart went an eternal abhorrence of sin and an ever-
increasing desire after a clean heart. 'An unbroken
heart, an high head, a tearless eye and an unbent
knee', was how a good man once described the Pharisee
praying in the temple beside the poor publican who,
like David, could only say, 'God be merciful to me a
sinner'.

The tears which flow from a broken and contrite
heart are precious to God. He puts them in His bottle.
The odour of penitence arising from the broken heart of
His people is sweet to God. In the words of a famous
divine: 'There is to the ear of God, more music in the
sighs of His people than in the songs of angels.' But the
day is coming when He shall wipe away all tears from
their eyes. And for ever and ever they shall bring their
sacrifices of praise to the Lamb who died that their sin
might be for ever put away.

'But I am like a green olive tree in the house of God'

Evil men are like thorns and briars. They may also grow 'like a green bay tree', assuming a momentary form of greatness, only to be 'soon cut down'. David, in all humility, and conscious of his union with God, put himself in a different category. 'I am like a green olive tree.' God had changed him. His spiritual roots were fixed in the One who said, 'From me is thy fruit found'. His spiritual resources were all derived from God alone.

The olive tree, naturally speaking, yielded three distinct blessings to man. It provided oil for the lamp; its fruits were nourishing and wholesome; and it had healing properties which often alleviated pain. What a true emblem of God's child this is! Because the oil of grace is in his soul he is, as Christ said of Himself, 'a light in the world'. With God's Word and life in his heart he can nourish the hungry soul. And by his sympathy and prayers he can bring comfort to those who mourn.

We have known some of Christ's poor ones who, after an hour of Christian fellowship, would remark, 'My soul is the better for being in your company'. This is what the Lord expects of each and all of us. 'Let your light so shine before men.' 'Feed my lambs.' 'Comfort ye, comfort ye, my people.' God's people are meant to communicate to one another the blessings they receive from Him. 'Come and hear, all ye that fear God, and I will declare what he hath done for my soul.'

To bear fruit, we must maintain our communion with Him. We must remain in that spiritual environment which is congenial to our spiritual growth. '*But I am like a green olive tree in the house of God.*' Our secret exercises at the throne of grace, our worship in our families or in the public means of grace, are God's house on earth. There, under the dew of His presence, our 'branches shall spread', and our 'beauty shall be as the olive tree'.

### PSALM 53: GOD'S CHILD IN A DEFILED WORLD
#### 'Corrupt are they'

Sometimes as we read our newspapers we are shocked at man's ever-deepening depravity. 'Evil men shall wax worse and worse.' Without exaggeration, our world is a moral dunghill, a place of defilement. We know, however, but very little of the world as it really is. Only an omniscient God knows all the actions, all the thoughts and all the secrets of men. 'I the Lord search the heart.' And in that heart He finds nothing but desperate and, apart from His own work of grace, incurable wickedness.

Out of the heart of men proceed all the evils which contaminate our world. The more we think of this the more we should wonder at God's forbearance and long-suffering. But to these there is a limit. He bore with the wickedness of the ancient world till humanity reached the point of no return. Then there was the Flood.

> *How in a moment suddenly*
> *To ruin brought are they!*
> *With fearful terrors utterly,*
> *They are consumed away.*

Talking about God's forbearance reminds us of a good man who was once going towards God's house on the Lord's Day. In the way he saw a number of men deliberately desecrating the day which God had appointed for man's rest and for His own worship. Righteous indignation moved his spirit as he said to them, 'Good it is for you that I am not God.'

One evidence of our spiritual change is that we keep ourselves unspotted from the world. Enoch kept himself unspotted from all the defilements of his age. He walked with God. The same **was** true of those few names in Sardis who had not defiled their garments, and to whom He gave the delightful promise that they would walk with Him in white. How careful we should be not to allow the least stain on the garments of our consecration to God!

PSALM 54: OUR SUPREME HELPER

'The Lord is with them that uphold my soul'

In the midst of all his afflictions David was aware not only of God's constant help, but also that there were those who fulfilled the law of Christ by bearing his burdens before the Lord in prayer and in other ways. The saints have communion with one another both in their sorrows and in their joys. We are commanded to lift up the hands which hang down, and the feeble knees. We give one or two instances of this.

# Psalm 54

In a certain city congregation there was a Christian woman who lived for many days under a heavy cloud of spiritual anxiety. One evening, outside the church door, a friend came up to her and quoted the words of Psalm 121: 'The Lord shall preserve thee from all evil: He shall preserve thy soul.' This proved to be a word in season. The clouds lifted and the Sun of righteousness arose again on her spirit with healing in His wings.

In that same congregation there was a man whose spiritual conflicts were very prolonged. But there were those who tried to uphold him by their prayers and Christian sympathy. One of these friends brought him a word which, by its effect on his spirit, he knew was from the Lord Himself:

> *His feathers shall thee hide; thy trust*
> *Under his wings shall be:*
> *His faithfulness shall be a shield*
> *And buckler unto thee.*

These words were like a leaf of healing from the tree of life. He knew also that, as the vast universe around him is upheld by the word of God's power, so, in all its feebleness, is the soul which is made a new creation in Christ. We are 'kept by the power of God'.

In a certain cemetery in America there is a memorial stone bearing the name of a good man who throughout his Christian life was conscious of his need of the grace that would enable him to persevere in God's way to the end. And under his name, one word only is inscribed – 'KEPT'. 'Hitherto hath the Lord helped us.'

These Psalms have one thing in common. In vivid language they present us with a view of David passing through some of his greatest afflictions. One of his natural, or instinctive, reactions to his sufferings was that he might 'get away from them all'. If only he had 'wings like a dove' that he might fly away to some place of rest, far beyond the reach of fear and danger! For God's people, however, confronted, as they often are, with many adverse providences, there is no such place in this lower vale. 'In this world ye shall have tribulation.'

God's people are often described in the Scriptures under this same lovely figure: 'Who are these that fly as a cloud, and as doves to their windows?' 'Though ye have lien among the pots, yet shall ye be as the wings of a dove covered with silver, and her feathers with yellow gold.' Christ addresses His bride in similar words: 'O my dove, that art in the clefts of the rock, in the secret places of the stairs, let me see thy countenance, let me hear thy voice.' But, like the dove that came back into the ark, not until life's storms all pass away shall they enter upon the final 'rest which remaineth for the people of God'.

David, we notice, discovered a more excellent way of easing his burden. 'Cast thy burden upon the Lord and he shall sustain thee.' This we do by bringing it to the Lord in prayer. In the original Hebrew the word 'burden' also means 'a gift'. Samuel Rutherford once wrote that when Christ espoused His people to Himself, one of His marriage gifts to each one of them was a cross. Some former Christians used to speak of their trials as 'the ballast in the boat', keeping the vessel steady and balanced. This is well illustrated in the case of Paul: 'Lest I should be exalted above measure through the abundance of the revelations, there was given to me a thorn in the flesh, the messenger of Satan to buffet me, lest I should be exalted above measure.' The thorn stayed with him. It kept him humble and dependent on the Lord to the end. Our pains and chastenings are among God's priceless gifts to us. Therefore, when we are inclined to say, 'My burden is more than I can bear', let us remember that our burdens are not more than He can bear. And with our burdens He carries ourselves as well. The wisdom of the saint consists in this: 'Casting all your care upon him, for he careth for you.'

### PSALM 57: 'THE SHADOW OF THY WINGS'

The earnest pleas of this Psalm emerged from the heart of David when he was in the cave of Adullam, and when Saul was seeking to take away his life. One of the mysteries of God's providence is seen in the way in which He permits that here His people should pass through many tribulations.

All God's people are conscious that they are beset by many dangers. If we bear the image of Christ in our walk and conversation, and if we seek to do His will, we shall discover that our enemies are many and that their hatred toward us is unremitting. Christ warned His people against misjudging the spirit of this world. 'Marvel not that the world hate you.' Our enemies are not only in the world, they are in hell; and, as we know, they are also, while sin remains, in our own hearts. Beyond the shadow of Saul, David could see the more menacing shadow of Satan – the lion of hell who would, if he could, have swallowed him up.

It is through the channel of our helplessness that God communicates His strength to us. In our spiritual warfare the smallest degree of self-sufficiency may stand as a barrier between us and His help. And it is by the door of self-confidence that Satan often brings us low. How vividly do we see this in the case of Peter. All might fail and deny the Lord, but not he. In his own strength he was going to follow Christ through every crisis and trial. But soon he found himself being sifted in Satan's sieve. How feeble he was in the hands of the enemy the moment he forgot that only in Christ's strength could he be safe! Here, then, is David in all his conscious weakness. But through faith and prayer help came to him from above. 'He shall send from heaven and save me from the reproach of him that would swallow me up. God shall send forth his mercy and his truth.' Above and beyond the power of darkness is 'the most High'. 'There is none like unto the God of Jeshurun, who rideth upon the heaven in thy help . . . The eternal God is thy refuge and underneath are the everlasting arms.' Christ has 'all power' in heaven and in earth and none ever perished who trusted in Him.

Not only did David's faith and prayers link themselves to God's power but also to His faithfulness. God had given him great and precious promises both within the sphere of providence and of grace. All his enemies were to be subdued. He was to prosper in his soul and his latter end was to be like a morning without a cloud, clothed in tranquillity and peace. But now he was imprisoned in a cave, a homeless wanderer, and surrounded by dark, frowning providences. There were moments in his stricken life when he let forth the cry, 'Lord, where are thy former lovingkindnesses which thou swearest unto David in thy truth?' But his faith was still unbroken. It was severely tried but not overcome. He knew that God would 'perform all things' for him. He who after many trials and long delays performed 'the truth to Jacob and the mercy to Abraham' was his God also. His covenant with him was 'ordered in all things and sure'. All things were ordained to work together for his good. If the Lord gave us His promise He will try our faith in the promise which He gives. But in the day of adversity we must not faint. If many clouds come between us and the stars which grace our sky, these will one day flee away for ever. True faith survives every test. David knew, however, that not till his pilgrimage here would end could he be free from affliction and danger. He therefore resolves to shelter under the wings of the Eternal. This is a figure which the Holy Spirit often uses in the Word to illustrate God's nearness to His people. It is also expressive of how God in all His attributes shields His people from the perils to which they are exposed. In another Psalm he says: 'Because thou hast been my help, therefore in the shadow of thy wings will I rejoice.' God, in other words, is the dwelling place, or the home, of the redeemed. 'Lord,' said Moses, 'thou hast been our dwelling place in all generations.' From all eternity they had a place in His love and in His purpose of grace.

'From everlasting to everlasting' He is their God. Under these wings the people of God are as safe as those who are already in heaven. This is the great assurance given to the Church in another Psalm. 'He that dwelleth in the secret place of the most High shall *abide* under the shadow of the Almighty. He is my refuge and my fortress: my God, in him will I trust.' 'The beloved of the Lord shall dwell *in safety* by him.' When Israel of old was passing through a great and terrible wilderness, the pillar of cloud by day and the pillar of fire by night was never withdrawn from them for a single moment. Christ entered our world that through His death on the cross He might for evermore be our hiding place. He is the cleft Rock of Ages in whom all His people find reconciliation, shelter and joy. When Ruth made choice of God and His people, Boaz addressed her in these lovely words: 'The Lord recompense thy work, and a full reward be given thee of the Lord God of Israel under whose wings thou art come to trust.' And under His wings we remain till all the calamities of life pass away.

### PSALMS 58–60: 'I WILL REJOICE'

There are those within God's family who deprive themselves of the comfort and joy which God's promises should impart to their souls. One of our great enemies is the sin of unbelief. We feel our own unworthiness. We say that our spot is not that of His children. As with many of God's saints, the evil thoughts and fiery darts with which Satan may invade our minds cast us down. We cannot dissociate these from our own nature, and we may conclude that if we were truly the Lord's we would have a greater degree of inner holiness. We may say: 'The promise cannot be mine. Those who have this treasure within their hearts are made vessels unto honour, but I am altogether as an unclean thing.'

Two men were once together on a journey. One was almost on the lap of despair. The comfort which he derived from God's Word in other days was no longer his. He would say: 'Mine iniquities have taken hold upon me, so that I am not able to look up.' Shortly before this good man passed into God's presence, he appeared to his friend in a vivid dream while a voice uttered the words: 'To this man will I look, even to him that is poor and of a contrite spirit, and trembleth at my word.' 'Poor John,' his friend whispered, 'will soon be beyond his fears.' And so it was. Within a short time he was in the upper sanctuary beholding the face of the One who loved him to the end.

We should never substitute our own feelings for what must always be the true foundation of our spiritual comfort. 'God hath spoken in his holiness, I will rejoice.' The God of infinite and unchangeable holiness 'is not a man that he should lie . . . Hath he said and shall he not do it? or hath he spoken and shall he not make it good?' All His promises to His people are like a nail in a sure place, confirmed by His oath.

When God gave His promise to Abraham that He would give him the land of Canaan for an inheritance, he was but one man, while the land which He had promised him was swarming with many thousands of those who knew not God. But God had spoken and Abraham rejoiced. He saw by faith the One through whom and in whom he was to obtain all his blessings on earth and in heaven. 'Abraham rejoiced to see my day: and he saw it and was glad.'

PSALMS 61–62: 'THE ROCK OF ISRAEL'
'He only is my rock'

One of the blasphemies of the Papal Church is seen in the way in which it endows mere men with names and a dignity which should be ascribed only to God. Simon Peter, they maintain, is the rock on which Christ founded His Church. If this were so, the rich and clear prophetic element in the Old Testament could not but make some mention of the fact; but on this claim the Scriptures are completely silent. The Holy Spirit in the Word never breathed one syllable in confirmation of such a claim. It is, therefore, a false claim, which Peter himself, in all his epistles inspired by that same Spirit, disowns and denies. In all the Psalms the word 'rock' is used only in relation to God in the Person of the Son. 'He *only* is my rock and my salvation.'

The Christ of God is the only foundation of the true Church. And because David's trust was wholly and eternally in Him, he could not be moved. The gates of hell can never prevail against those who rest on Christ alone for salvation.

This Rock is also the Church's refuge: 'God is a refuge for us.' 'A man shall be as an hiding place from the wind, and a covert from the tempest . . . and as the shadow of a great rock in a weary land.' 'The man Christ Jesus.'

> *Rock of Ages, cleft for me,*
> *Let me hide myself in Thee.*

Christ is also the smitten Rock out of which flows the river of life. The Rock which follows the Church in every age is Christ.

In another Psalm the Lord reminds Israel of how, if only they had obeyed His voice, He would have fed them with 'honey out of the rock'. In other words, Christ has a fullness of truth. The written Word is Christ's mouth which to His Church 'is most sweet'. 'Thy words were found and I did eat them; and thy word was unto me the joy and rejoicing of mine heart.' To the hungry soul it is 'sweeter than honey and the dropping of honeycombs'.

In his song [*Deut* 32] Moses speaks of Israel as having sucked honey and oil out of the rock. Oil, as we said before, was a source of light. So Christ is the fountain of light. In Him was life and His life was the light of men. The two go together – life and light! 'The Lord is my light and my salvation.'

God put Moses into the cleft of a rock where he was given a view of His glory. Otherwise stated, it is in Christ alone that we behold God's glory. 'No man hath seen God at any time; the only begotten Son who is in the bosom of the Father, he hath declared [or revealed] him.'

What are the consequences of rejecting or neglecting Christ as the sole source and foundation of man's happiness and safety? In answer we quote the Lord's own words: 'And whosoever shall fall on this stone shall be broken; but on whomsoever it shall fall, it will grind him to powder.' Let this, therefore, be our prayer: 'Lord, give me the wisdom to say, He only is my rock and my salvation.'

PSALMS 63–64: RETAINING OUR NEARNESS TO GOD
'My soul followeth hard after thee'

There are several types of men and women within the visible Church. There are those who follow Christ nominally, or from wrong motives. The foolish virgins were apparently sincere followers of Christ; but their attachment to Him was only in name. They knew not the Lord and the Lord knew not them. Like those in the Church at Sardis, they had a name to live but were dead. There were many who followed our Lord in the days of His flesh, but when the hour of sifting came, they moved away.

Among true Christians there are those who, in seasons of backsliding or decline, follow Him, like Peter on one occasion, 'afar off'. And there are those who, in storm and sunshine, cleave to Him, and enjoy daily communion with Him. Asaph could say amid all his perplexities: 'Nevertheless, I am continually with thee.' 'I held him,' said the Church, 'and I would not let him go.' It was she of whom the question was asked, 'Who is this that cometh up from the wilderness leaning upon her beloved?' Nearer to Him she could not be.

I once read the life-story of a true man of God. In the book the remark was made that for several years before he left this world he continually enjoyed God's sensible presence in his soul. Later I met an eminent father in Christ – Principal John Macleod – who told me that his own excellent wife, during her last year in this world was, night and day, blessed with the same awareness of God's nearness to her. But this we cannot retain with our arms folded or with our knees unbent, and in a state of spiritual slumber. In his spiritual exercises David did not halt in the way; and the One to whom he cleaved renewed his strength day by day.

They say that certain Orientals, when travelling, do not sit or lie down till they reach their journey's end. They run, and then they walk for a while till their strength is, in a measure, renewed. This fact elucidates the words found in Isaiah: 'But they that wait upon the Lord shall renew their strength . . . they shall run and not be weary; they shall walk and not faint.'

'My soul followeth hard after *thee*.' In other words, God is all the desire of His people. He is the subject of their love above and beyond all others.

A godly woman, who had lost both her husband and her only child, was dying. Both, she knew, had gone to be with Christ in heaven. Her love to them within the bonds of nature and grace was deep and constant. As she was leaving the world a friend said to her, 'Soon you will see them both.' Her answering words, which were also her last, were: 'Jesus first.' 'Whom I shall see for myself, and mine eyes shall behold, *and not another.*'

### PSALM 65: THE CROWN OF GOODNESS
'Thou crownest the year with thy goodness'

The world of nature has its different seasons. In the springtime we sow our seed. Soon the flowers are in their bud. The day lengthens and the air becomes warmer. The spirit of the creature becomes happier as nature again begins to smile. The springtime is quietly dovetailed into the summer months when nature is decked in her finest robe. Then, and all too soon, comes the season of maturity, when the corn and the fruit of the earth ripen, and when God crowns the year with His goodness.

Is there a spiritual parallel to this? Indeed there is; not only in the life of the Church of Christ, but also in the life of Christ Himself. It was through His coming into the world that the day-spring from on high visited us. It marked the dawn of a never-ending day for all His people. For thirty years our Lord lived a quiet and holy life in constant communion with the Father, in whose bosom He dwelt from all eternity. Then came what one might call the winter storms of sufferings, rejection and death. For this end He came into the world, that He might suffer and die, the Just in the room of the unjust. But those awful agonies were followed by a lovely spiritual summer. If His sun went down in a sea of wrath, it arose again to go down no more. His resurrection and exaltation commenced the season of unending joy for Himself and for all His people. It was for the joy set before Him that He endured the cross and despised the shame. This joy His people shall share. 'And they returned to Jerusalem with *great* joy, and were *continually* in the temple praising and blessing God.' 'He shall see of the travail of His soul and shall be satisfied.' A great multitude which no man can number shall for ever sing His praise. The first verse of this Psalm tells us: 'Praise waiteth for thee, O God, in Zion.'

> *Within the congregation great,*
> *My praise shall be of thee.*

These seasons in the life of our Lord are also, though in a minor and different way, reproduced in the experience of His people. By His Spirit He calls them out of the grasp of death and out of the grip of their spiritual winter. How beautifully put are His own words on this theme: 'Rise up, my love, my fair one, and come away. For lo, the winter is past, the rain is over and gone, the flowers appear on the earth, the time of the singing of birds is come, and the voice of the turtle is heard in our land.' All who serve the Lord and suffer for Him have the promise that they shall 'reap with joy and return bringing their sheaves with them'. The joy of harvest!

'For thou, O God, hast proved us: Thou hast tried us as
silver is tried'

These words imply that pain is a necessary accompani-
ment of our sanctification. God has chosen His people
in the furnace of affliction, and in that furnace He
often leaves them till they are made perfect in holiness.
He has 'his fire in Sion and his furnace in Jerusalem'.
But, O what care He exercises over them as they pass
through the process of pain! His eye is constantly upon
them. He will not try them beyond what they can
endure. 'And he shall sit as a refiner and purifier of
silver; and he shall purify the sons of Levi, and purge
them as gold and silver, that they may offer unto the
Lord an offering in righteousness.' He is not standing
or passing by them now and again, but sitting with His
watchful and loving eye upon them all. In fact He
Himself is with them in every furnace of trial. 'In all
their afflictions he was afflicted.' The three young
men who were cast into the furnace in Babylon had
the Lord Himself as their companion in their sufferings.

When Saul of Tarsus sought to destroy His people,
He said, 'Saul, Saul, why persecutest thou *me*?' Who
can understand how tender, intimate and personal is
the tie between Christ and His mystical body, the
Church? The Apostle Peter, whom Satan – permitted
by Christ to try His servant – desired to sift as wheat,
knew that God's people in every age would, in one form
or another, be subject to the same or similar trials.
Therefore, he wrote these precious words: 'Beloved,
think it not strange concerning the fiery trial which is
to try you, as though some strange thing happened
unto you; but rejoice, inasmuch as ye are partakers of

[113]

Christ's sufferings; that, when his glory shall be revealed, ye may be glad also with exceeding joy.'

It is said that in the ancient world the refiner would not cease his process of purification until he saw his own image perfectly reflected in the contents of his vessel. And all the heirs of salvation, who come out of great tribulation, shall be presented to their Lord without spot, and satisfied with His likeness. 'Thou broughtest us into a wealthy place', where all pain, mental, spiritual or physical, is unknown. Heaven is the abode of eternal peace.

## PSALMS 67–68: GOD'S MIGHTY ARMY
'Great was the company of those who published it'

The Gospel is glad tidings of great joy. The new man in Christ is given new spiritual perceptions whereby he comes to know something of the glory and unspeakable blessings of the Gospel. He tastes of Christ's love. He hears His voice, a voice without comparison in heaven or on earth. He makes a discovery of God's loving and sovereign interest in man, and of the joy and blessedness of knowing Him. He reads in God's Word of the unending happiness reserved for all who love Him. All this fills him with wonder. He would communicate his knowledge of Christ and His great salvation to his fellow-men. Like many in other ages, God may specifically call him to proclaim His Gospel to a lost world. The Lord said of Saul, 'He is a chosen vessel unto me, to bear my name before the Gentiles and kings and the children of Israel'. 'We cannot but speak the things which we have seen and heard.' 'If these should hold their peace, the stones would immediately cry out.' 'Ye are my witnesses, saith the Lord.'

In the Scottish Highlands a man could be seen walking along the road with a Bible in his hand. His name was Finlay Munro. In his day the Gospel had not yet been proclaimed in the Western Isles, and a burden was resting on his mind to tell his fellow-sinners of God's salvation. In the Island of Lewis he climbed a little hill, and thousands of men and women came to listen to his words. He gave out his text: 'In this mountain shall the Lord of hosts make unto all people a feast of fat things, a feast of wines on the lees, of fat things full of marrow, of wines on the lees well refined.' Many were brought to Christ that day. The word was with power. Many years afterwards two men sat on the top of that same hill. They recalled that day of long ago, and together they sang a Psalm:

> *Of corn an handful in the earth*
> *On tops of mountains high,*
> *With prosperous fruit shall shake, like trees*
> *On Lebanon that be.*

The two men knew something of the great cloud of witnesses who could directly or indirectly trace their salvation to that memorable day. But the herald of God was only one of many throughout the land who had gone to the distant places of the earth with the 'good news from a far country'.

In this our own day, when Satan and evil men are spewing out of their mouths a flood of errors, let us pray that many may arise who shall serve Him and who shall again proclaim 'the faith once delivered to the saints'. Let us pray for the day when the false and foul tongue shall be put to silence, and when the true Church of God, in her warfare against evil, shall once more become 'terrible as an army with banners'.

PSALM 69: 'REPROACH HATH BROKEN MY HEART'

Although some of the adverse experiences mentioned in this Psalm were related to the life of David, it is equally obvious that it touches depths of sorrow which can only apply to a greater than David, even the eternal Son of God. Literally speaking, Christ died of a broken heart. As, in His holy nature and sinless life, He came into opposition to a godless and God-hating world, to sin in all its malevolence, and to the temptations of Satan, sorrow crushed His heart. Men blasphemed His name. All the sins and sorrows of His people were put into His cup. No sooner did the Father announce that He was His beloved Son, than hell and all the forces of darkness were on the alert. Satan immediately came to Him as a spirit of reproach and blasphemy. 'All these things will I give thee if thou wilt fall down and worship me.' Although Satan left Christ for a season, his malicious eye was on Him to the end. And many were Satan's tools to misrepresent and distress His holy life. In Judas Iscariot he had his representative within the circle of the apostles. 'Have not I chosen you twelve,' said Christ, 'and one of you is a devil?'

Many of God's people, in a lesser degree, partake of the sufferings of Christ. With John Bunyan, James Fraser of Brea, C. H. Spurgeon, John Love, and many others, we believe that there are no sufferings peculiar to the Christian life more difficult to endure than those which are occasioned by men who pour scorn on the Being and glory of God Himself. With comparative ease we can usually endure Satan's false accusations against ourselves, for often he has much whereof to accuse us. But when He reproaches and blasphemes the holy Name of Him whose honour and glory we place infinitely beyond that of any other, our heart is crushed and our spirit is broken. The more we love God, the deeper Satan's hatred toward us will become. His most fiery darts are reserved for those who put God's honour first.

In these conflicts we can only say, 'The Lord rebuke thee, Satan'. We can only resort to Him who is a refuge from the storm and who went through these storms Himself. 'He is my refuge and my fortress: my God; in him will I trust.'

And soon our warfare shall end to recur no more. 'We are more than conquerors through him who loved us' and 'the God of peace shall bruise Satan under your feet shortly'.

We begin our life in a state of feebleness and entire dependence, and we may end it on the lap of infirmity and helplessness. The Psalm speaks of these two states. 'By thee have I been holden up from the womb.' 'Now also, when I am old and grey-headed, O God, forsake me not.' God's love towards His people is seen in His continual care for them from the moment they enter the world till they draw their last breath. 'Hearken unto me, O house of Jacob . . . which are carried [by me] from the womb: and even to your old age I am he; and even to hoar hairs will I carry you . . .'

When our strength is abated in this way, symptoms that our end is approaching begin to show themselves. The eye becomes dim. The step is slower. The breath becomes shorter. Some years ago I stood by the bed of an old Christian minister. In my prayer I quoted the words: 'My flesh and my heart faileth: but God is the strength of my heart and my portion for ever.' Immediately he was in a state of joy and great spiritual comfort. The end was near, but the Lord who was his portion upheld him by His word till he entered glory.

The Psalmist desired that God would still spare him that he might continue to witness for Him in this world. Life in retrospect can be full of regret. We look back on days of spiritual leanness and unprofitable service. We have done so little for the One who has ever been our help and who loves us to the end.

In the previous Psalm David speaks of himself as being poor and needy, but to the end his resolve was: 'I will go on in the strength of the Lord.' The day of weakness had arrived, but he knew the promise: 'As thy days, so shall thy strength be.'

I cannot deny but that this is one of my favourite Psalms; not because of its sublime poetry or personal associations, but by reason of its rich promises and glorious prophetic optimism. One of my treasured memories is that of sitting as a young boy in a church in the Outer Hebrides. The evening was lovely beyond words, with the moon and the stars adorning the night sky. The minister gave out the Psalm and the congregation began to sing:

> To him that made the great lights shine:
>     For mercy hath he ever.
> The sun to rule till day decline;
>     For his grace faileth never.
>
> The moon and stars to rule by night:
>     For mercy hath he ever.

Another memory is that of sitting in a church in Glasgow. The Lord was truly among us. A young man, with a voice of surpassing power and melody, led the praise:

> They shall thee fear while sun and moon
>     Do last through ages all.
> Like rain on mown grass he shall drop,
>     Or show'rs on earth that fall.

There was another night when, sitting in our manse in Resolis, I felt very discouraged at the state of God's cause, and over the departure of those witnesses who graced the firmament of the Church in other days. Then I moved outside. The sky was ablaze with stars, while the moon beamed on the silent woods and harvest fields nearby. It was then that these same words arrested my mind: 'They shall fear thee as long as the sun and the moon endure, throughout all generations.' The Lord, I knew, has had His witnesses in this world from the days of Abel till the present moment. And the future was bright with many promises of better days. The Prince of Peace, I knew, was sitting on His throne in heaven; 'His name shall endure for ever,' and there shall be for all who love Him, 'abundance of peace so long as the moon endureth.' That night, as I looked towards the heavens, I also recalled God's promise to Abraham, 'So shall thy seed be'.

But my greatest joy came through the knowledge that all the people of God who in every generation were spiritual lights in this world were shining more gloriously in that world wherein dwelleth righteousness. 'And they that be wise shall shine as the brightness of the firmament, and they that turn many to righteousness as the stars for ever and ever'. I knew also that, throughout her history, the Church of God, like the moon, did wax and wane, but that her most glorious hour in this world is yet to be. 'Who is she that looketh forth as the morning, fair as the moon, clear as the sun, and terrible as an army with banners?'

PSALM 73: WHERE TO GO WITH OUR TROUBLES
'It is good for me to draw near to God'

Like Asaph in this Psalm, all of us, at one time or another, have grave problems to face. These may be personal to ourselves, or they may be related to a wider providential sphere. God's providence is a great deep. He may conceal from us, as in the case of Daniel, 'the end of these things'. He may, on the other hand, as He did in the case of Asaph, throw a flood of light on what is yet to come. Where should we go with our greatest problems? For those who are wise, there are supremely, but two places to which they may resort – the Bible and the throne of grace. The Bible is a revelation of God's mind! In the days of Asaph this revelation was still unfolding. Now it is final.

Just as the Queen of Sheba came to Solomon with all her 'hard questions', we should bring them all before the Lord at the throne of grace. The Lord, in His wisdom may not see fit to resolve, or ease us of, all these. He may have something better in store for us, by giving us the grace of patience and resignation. He will cause us to know that our present trials are infinitely preferable to the best that wicked man can possess in this life. Their little heaven, as the Psalm proclaims, lies on the brink of woe, while our time of 'sorrow and sighing' is but for a moment and only a step from the heavenly Canaan. He will also enable us to see that 'through each perplexing path of life' He is our unfailing guide, and that the day is coming when 'He shall bring forth thy righteousness as the light and thy judgment as the noonday'.

Such a sure hope should enable us to say with another, 'Lord, let me drink the waters of Marah as long as they are sweetened by thy promise'.

'O deliver not the soul of thy turtle dove unto the
multitude of the wicked'

When Christ addresses His Church as His 'dove' He is
not only using a term of endearment, but He is also
describing her in her holy simplicity, her purity of life
and her constant need of protection. Her survival in a
God-hating world is one evidence of His care of her.
Because she bears His image and obeys His voice she
also is hated. 'Ye shall be hated of all men for my
name's sake.' This is an hostility which God's people
have encountered in every age. It began with Abel and
it will so continue till the last of Christ's loved ones is
taken Home. It is not something which invariably
proceeds from the external irreligious world; it may
also come from those who are found within the Church.
Our Lord challenged the orthodox Pharisees of His
own day to mention even one of God's prophets whom
their fathers had not persecuted or slain. They themselves were the vicious men who, in malice, condemned
Him to the death of the Cross. 'They hated me without
a cause.'

In all the apostolic epistles, warnings are given of a
coming false Church which, by its wiles and pretentions,
will parade itself as the true Church and persecute the
godly. Nothing has appeared on the scene which
answers to this terrifying picture but the papal system.
The pages of history show that all who adhered to
God's Word, or to the testimony of Jesus Christ, became
the subjects of its hatred. 'And in her was found the
blood of prophets, and of saints, and of all that were
slain upon the earth.'

In the present hour we see a great evil rearing its

ugly head and threatening to put 'the remnant that remains' of God's true witnesses out of existence. It is the combination of apostate churches which have wandered far from the Reformed witness and which are seeking 'ecumenical unity' with the papal system. Many are being caught in this snare. Our Lord predicted that the day would come when many false Christs and false prophets would arise who would, if it were possible, deceive the very elect. One major aim of this gigantic and deceptive movement is to silence the voice of Christ's dove, the voice of those who preach the Word of God in its purity. What should be our prayer in such an hour? 'Arise, O God, plead thine own cause.' And what is our comfort? 'If God be for us, who can be against us?' 'No weapon that is formed against thee shall prosper; and every tongue that shall rise against thee in judgment thou shalt condemn. This is the heritage of the servants of the Lord, and their righteousness is of me, saith the Lord.'

### PSALMS 75–76: GOD'S REVERSING ACTS
'He putteth down one, and setteth up another'

History is replete with the stories of men who tried to set themselves up, even above the God of Heaven. Pharaoh reacted to God's command to let his people go by saying, 'Who is God that I should obey him?' Nebuchadnezzar endeavoured to set his throne and kingdom above Him whose throne and kingdom are for ever and ever. Herod listened to the adulations of his degenerate admirers: 'It is the voice of a god and not of a man.' Coming nearer to our own time, we have read of how Adolph Hitler gazed at a picture of himself riding proudly on a white horse, a picture which bore the blasphemous title: 'In the Beginning was the Word.' Then in a voice that deliberately mocked Christ, the Eternal King, he exclaimed – 'I am providence'. But Pharaoh and his hosts are swept to destruction; Nebuchadnezzar becomes a companion of 'the beasts of the field'; Herod is devoured by worms and Hitler becomes a suicide. 'Those that walk in pride God is able to abase.' 'He shall cut off the spirit of princes: he is terrible to the kings of the earth.' 'All the horns of the wicked will I cut off.'

The greatest punishment and humiliation of all is yet to be meted out to a man whose head bears 'the names of blasphemy' and whose so-called Church is yet to be made to drink '*the cup of the wine of the fierceness* of God's wrath'. There are few predictive words in the Bible more terrible than these.

But look at the other side of the picture. 'He setteth up another.' There is another King whose glory is without compare. He is indeed 'the King of glory'. He was here among us 'without form or comeliness . . . that we should desire him'. It was He who said: 'But I am a worm, and no man; a reproach of men, and despised of the people.' He was 'the stone which the builders rejected'. And who were His followers? Listen to the voices of one or two of the greatest among them: 'He must increase but I must decrease.' 'This is a faithful saying, and worthy of all acceptation that

Jesus Christ came into the world to save sinners, of whom I am chief.'

During my college days there was one student among us who lived very near the Lord. One day he said to a friend who stood beside him: 'There is only one man in this college of whose godliness I stand in doubt.' 'And who might he be?' he was asked. 'Myself, myself,' was the answer. True saints are always 'lowly in heart.'

At God's right hand now sits our glorified Redeemer 'crowned with many crowns'. And His promise to all His lowly ones runs thus:

> *He from the dust doth raise the poor*
> *That very low doth lie;*
> *And from the dunghill lifts the man*
> *Oppressed with poverty;*
>
> *That he may highly him advance,*
> *And with the princes set;*
> *With those that of his people are*
> *The chief, ev'n princes great.*

PSALMS 77–78: 'THOU LEDDEST THY PEOPLE'

The closing verses of these two Psalms speak of Moses and David as faithful men whom God had set apart to care for His people in this world. They were, however, but pale types of Him who is supremely 'the Good Shepherd'. Besides, their tenure of office in this capacity was for a brief hour, while His is eternal. 'The Lord is my shepherd.' Few, if any, words in the

Bible touch our hearts like these. Books have been written on the tenderness, the mysteriousness and intimacy of the link between the Oriental shepherd and his flock. The tie of love, sympathy and knowledge between Christ and His flock, however, no one can describe. 'It passeth knowledge.' And what precious memories and experiences we could weave around these words – 'my shepherd'! Are you a lamb – timid, halting and weary? Do not forget that, perhaps unknown to yourself, you are in His bosom. His eye is upon you night and day. His rod and staff shall ward off every foe and guide you to the end. Are you old and stricken in years, weary in the way, and about to cross the last river which separates you from the land of your desire? Then sit down and ponder on these words, 'Hitherto hath the Lord helped us'. Is not your life a miracle of preservation? His promise, like a star, has guided you through every dark hour, while His goodness and mercy have followed you all your days. 'But,' you ask, 'how will it fare with me in the swellings of Jordan?'

My late beloved father once stood at the bedside of a dear man of God who was dying. In answer to the question as to how he felt, he replied: 'I am now crossing the river, but I have no awareness of it, for He is with me.' Often I have come across those who delight to hear their favourite verses being sung. They belong to the Psalm:

> *But His own people, like to sheep,*
> *Thence to go forth he made;*
> *And he, amidst the wilderness,*
> *Them, as a flock, did lead.*

*To borders of his sanctuary*
*The Lord his people led,*
*Ev'n to the mount which his right hand*
*For them had purchased.*

None of His people will be missing in the day when He makes up His jewels. It was the famous Lachlan Mackenzie who once said that if even one of His people were missing on the last day, Christ would turn the universe upside down till that one was safe in the heavenly fold. 'Behold, I and the children whom God hath given me.'

PSALMS 79–80: 'TURN US AGAIN'

Is there anything in the history of mankind more tragic than the story of the Jewish race? God embraced them tenderly within His covenant. The covenant which He made with Abraham He also made with his seed. It was not because they were superior to all other races that God made choice of them. 'The Lord did not set his love upon you, nor choose you, because ye were more in number than any people ... but because the Lord loved you, and because he would keep the oath which he had sworn unto your fathers ...'

Moses, who uttered these words, spent many days warning Israel of the dire consequences of dishonouring or rejecting their God. But reject Him they did. This reached its dread climax when they cried: 'Away with him. Let him be crucified.' Their Messiah had come. He had told them that He was the God of Abraham. 'Before Abraham was, I AM.' Moses not only warned them of the physical sufferings in which their rejection of their Messiah would involve them, but also of their spiritual plight. The Psalm speaks of these.

For hundreds of years the history of Israel has been one of deep sorrow. Nor has Europe's boasted civilization brought an end to their sufferings. Only a few years ago millions of Jews were driven into gas chambers or shut up in concentration camps of deepest horror. Moses had told them of dreadful terrors to come, both physical and spiritual. The Lord Himself shed tears over their doomed city. Paul the apostle experienced 'great heaviness and continual sorrow' of heart over their sad plight. The consequences of unbelief are indeed tragic in the extreme. The apostle speaks of them 'filling up their sins alway: for the wrath is come upon them to the uttermost.'

But from Israel we turn again to think of our own day and nation. It is easy to alienate God's presence from our midst; but it is not so easy to get Him back again. Over a hundred years ago a minister of God who had laboured over the years in the Scottish Highlands said, 'I am happy that I had a glimpse of the Ark of God in these parts before it vanished out of sight.' Many years afterwards, in a community where farming was the principal occupation of the people, another minister asked what would have happened if not a shower of rain had fallen on the land for over a hundred years. Just what? Spiritually speaking, this has happened. God turns 'a fruitful land into barrenness for the wickedness of them that dwell therein'. Places in our country which were once the gardens of the Lord have become spiritual graveyards.

Are we aware of this calamity? If so, let us also pray with the Psalmist: 'Let thy hand be upon the man of thy right hand, upon the son of man whom thou madest strong for thyself . . . Turn us again, O Lord God of hosts, cause thy face to shine; and we shall be saved.' It is in answer to prayer that the Lord is going to turn the captivity of Israel, and to revive those nations which at the moment are pining away because God's Spirit is absent. When this happens, the desert will again rejoice and blossom as the rose.

PSALM 81: GOD'S FEAST FOR HIS POOR ONES
'Open thy mouth wide, and I will fill it'

One mark of all new creatures in Christ is that they are born into God's kingdom conscious of need. It is the poor in spirit who are destined to inherit the unsearchable riches of Christ. Here they 'hunger and thirst after righteousness'. All their well-springs are in God. Their mouths are, therefore, open before Him in continuous prayer: 'Give us this day our daily bread.'

And they are a people who come to God with great requests. They open their mouths *wide*. They covet earnestly the best gifts. Their spiritual aspirations, desires and requests embrace the eternal world and all the great and precious promises given by God in His Word. They hunger after all the blessings which make up the great feast reserved for them in heaven and of which they have a foretaste here.

Not only do they open their mouth wide but they open it often. 'Pray without ceasing.' Their sense of need deepens day by day. Therefore they are ever looking to the One who is able to supply all their needs according to His riches in glory by Christ Jesus.

And what is the promise? 'And I will fill it.' Christ sometimes brings us into His banqueting house and fills us with good things. A gracious woman once sat in a church and listened to a sermon which brought her much blessing. Then, as if speaking to the Lord, she whispered, 'Oh, withhold thine hand, for this clay vessel has more than it can hold'. If for His poor ones the crumbs which now fall from His table are so sweet and nourishing, how much more will the table above be where 'they shall hunger no more, neither thirst any more'.

### PSALMS 82–83: 'THY HIDDEN ONES'

While, on the one hand, our Lord commands that our light should shine before men and that we should be His epistles 'known and read of all men', on the other hand He knows how to hide us in the day of peril. These two Psalms were written in days of grave crises when, indeed, men had joined together to blot out God's name and to destroy His people. His command to His people was: 'Come, my people, enter thou into thy chambers, and shut thy doors about thee; hide thyself as it were for a little moment, until the indignation be overpast.' God was to bring His and their enemies under judgment; but His own people He was to preserve.

In the days of Elijah the Lord informed His servant that, unknown to him, He had seven thousand in Israel who had not bowed the knee to Baal or kissed his image. These were God's saints, hidden from the murderous Jezebel. In Europe, during centuries of papal darkness, God had His hidden ones in every nation. They were men and women who were waiting for the dawn of that day which came with the glorious Reformation.

I recently read a book entitled *Tortured for Christ*. It is the story of the hidden or underground witness and activities of God's persecuted saints under the Communist tyranny. It is also the story of mental and physical sufferings inflicted on them by the enemies of God. The spirit of atheism is the spirit of evil. The most wonderful part of the story has to do with the heavenly joy which reigned in the hearts of these dear men and women of God as they suffered for the witness of Jesus.

There are many instances in the Bible, and in the history of the Church, of God miraculously shielding His people in their hour of danger. How wonderfully is this seen, for example, in the lives of Abraham, Jacob, David, Elijah, Elisha and Paul. It is something which continues. During the first world war a friend of mine once found himself surrounded by wicked men whom he had rebuked for their misbehaviour. They told him that he had but one minute to live. As he waited for the end he shut his eyes for a moment and asked God to shield him. When he opened his eyes, he found that his would-be murderers had crawled away. It was something he could never explain. God often moves and performs His wonders in 'a mysterious way'. The 'miraculous' element does not often enter the context of normal Christian experience; but 'all his saints are in his hand' and 'the beloved of the Lord shall dwell in safety by him'.

There is another sense in which God's people are sometimes 'hidden ones'; they may be placed by their Lord under a blanket of obscurity or infirmity. He has chosen 'things which are not', or which are too mean in the eyes of the world to be taken notice of. In the place where I now labour there are several choice saints laid aside and of whose existence, and especially their godliness, only a few care to know. They are not of this world but belong to the people of whom it is said, 'The Lord knoweth them that are his'.

### PSALM 84: 'THE VALLEY OF BACA'

While Israel was on pilgrimage to the land of promise, God's presence among them was their guiding star in the way. Between them and their final place of rest lay the valley of Baca. It is a valley through which all true pilgrims pass.

The word 'Baca' means 'weeping'. From what sources do their sorrows arise? They certainly participate in the afflictions which are common to all men. But they have sorrows of which the world knows nothing. They

weep over the plague of their heart. As with Israel of
old, their grief, or cause of weeping, often comes
through the recollection of their past sins. They grieve
over their many lapses through their lack of vigilance
and the temptations of Satan, even as Peter wept
bitterly over his denial of his Lord. Like their Lord,
they weep over the sins of their age and the way in
which God's Word and law are despised and desecrated.

They are not, however, an idle people. Their sorrows
drive them to God's throne of grace. The grace which
is in their heart is in exercise. Their sorrows often cause
them to make greater discoveries of God's love and grace.
It is a grace which never fails or lets them down. 'My
grace is sufficient for you'. It is grace which is un-
brokenly linked with eternal glory. Such pilgrims,
then, must 'go from strength to strength', or as the
words may also mean, 'from company to company'. In
their sorrows they have fellowship with those who
know something of 'the afflictions of Joseph'.

A young man was once asked what united his heart
more than anything else to God's people. 'It was,' he
said, 'the discovery that what gave me grief of heart
was in their cup also.' The communion of saints has
its waters of Marah as well as its cup of consolation.

But 'at morn doth joy arise'. 'Every one of them in
Zion appeareth before God.'

I once attended a prayer meeting at which only one man was present. The rest were good Christian women. A few days afterwards, and in the same area, about two hundred men gathered round the grave of a fellow-farmer. The dead were there burying their dead, but few of them had any concern for God's diminished cause. It was so in other days as well. 'There is none that calleth upon thy name, that stirreth up himself to take hold of thee.' 'By whom,' asked the prophet, 'shall Jacob arise? for he is small.' Only Jacob's God can raise up Jacob from his low estate. 'Wilt *thou* not revive us again?'

The great revivals of the past were always preceded by the prayers of the Church, however small in number. Often they were 'the two or three'. In the Song of Solomon we hear the voice of the Bride in prayer: 'Awake, O north wind, and come thou south; blow upon my garden.' It was when, on God's instruction, the prophet prayed for the living breath that the miracle of life happened in the valley of dry bones. The great Pentecostal shower which descended upon the Church and on the world came in answer to the prayers of those who waited for the promise of the Father.

About fifty years ago a young minister was settled in a large Scottish congregation. Among the people there were those who were wrestling with God in prayer that his ministry would be blessed in the conversion of sinners. Before long there was the sound of an abundance of rain. Hard hearts were broken and dry eyes were filled with tears as they listened to God's Word preached in the power of the Spirit. In that place the Lord reaped an abundant harvest. The story is told of another community where a small number of God's people met in prayer. Late one night, before they separated, they sang a Psalm:

> *As Hermon's dew, the dew that doth*
> *On Sion's hills descend;*
> *For there the blessing God commands,*
> *Life that shall never end.*

God answered their prayers in the salvation of many souls. Such events are associated with great joy. It is a joy which is shared by the hosts of heaven. 'There is joy in the presence of the angels of God over one sinner that repenteth.' There is also joy on earth. 'When the Lord turned again the captivity of Zion, we were like them that dream. Then was our mouth filled with laughter and our tongue with singing.' God's Zion became a joyful mother of sons.

PSALM 86: 'A TOKEN FOR GOOD'

We knew a man who once prayed that the Lord might show him some token for good. A few nights afterwards he dreamt that he was in the company of old friends, some of whom had gone to their eternal Home. In conversation with one of them he was reminded that the greatest token for good that the Lord would ever show His people was Christ dying for them on the Cross. When he awoke he felt both rebuked and humbled.

As we read these words, we think perhaps of the tokens for good with which the father rejoiced the soul of the prodigal son when he found his way back to his home. He anticipated a deserved word of displeasure, if not of rejection, from the one against whom he had so grievously sinned. Instead of this a warm welcome awaited him. The father rejoices in the return of the lost one. The kiss of welcome, the best robe, the shoes, the ring, the feast of gladness, illustrate point by point the wonderful provisions found in the Gospel of the grace of God. Nothing is lacking that the penitent sinner needs. All is the Heavenly Father's free gift to him:

> *God of the covenant, Triune Jehovah,*
> *Marvels of mercy adoring we see:*
> *Seeker of souls, in the counsels eternal,*
> *Binding Thy lost ones for ever to Thee.*

The tokens for good which the Lord shows His people are beyond calculation. 'They are more than can be numbered.' This Psalm tells us of the hard things and bitter drops which were in David's cup at the time of its composition. Yet they were tokens for good. 'Whom the Lord loveth he chasteneth, and scourgeth every son whom he receiveth.' 'As many as I love I rebuke and chasten.'

Let us always remind ourselves that no favour, whether sweet or bitter, shall ever reach us but through the death of the Lamb of God. Throughout eternity He, and He alone, will therefore be the subject of His people's praise.

'The Lord shall count, when he writeth up the people,
that this man was born there'

This Psalm is prophetic. It anticipates the days when
heathen peoples would find their way into the Church
of God. 'Shall a nation be born at once?' This has happened in the past. The history of the Church from the
day of Pentecost till the time of the Reformation and
of the Great Evangelical Revival furnishes us with
striking fulfilments of this prophecy. And better days
are yet to come, days when our world shall resound with
the song, 'Hallelujah, for the Lord God omnipotent
reigneth'.

We notice in this Psalm God's act in writing down
each soul who is born into His kingdom. So precious is
their salvation to Him that He does not leave this to
men or angels, for only He knows all those who are His.
He knows where and when, in the mysteriousness of
His own work of regeneration, they pass from death to
life. We speak with all reverence when we say that He
is the heavenly Registrar in whose Book of Life are to be
found the names of all who belong to the Church of the
first-born.

We observe also that, although their regeneration has
its source in His own sovereign grace and power, the
Church, or His Sion, is mentioned as one of His choice
instruments in bringing souls to Himself, both through
her spiritual travail and her proclamation of His
Gospel.

There are some of God's people who cannot name the
day of their spiritual birth, or the time when they
were reborn of the Spirit of God. But He knows. It
has often been said that you need not know the hour or

day, or even the year, of your birth, to prove that you are alive. It is the same in the spiritual world. The important thing is that we bear the marks of His children; 'who were born, not of blood, nor of the will of the flesh, nor of the will of man, but of God'. Of His fullness they all receive 'and grace for grace'. 'As new-born babes they desire the sincere milk of the Word' that they may grow thereby.

### PSALM 88: 'THE LOWEST PIT'

Some of the Psalms touch the very heights of Christian consolation. Others describe the depths of sorrow into which God's children may sometimes come. At the Cross of Calvary, Christian, Bunyan's pilgrim, rejoiced with joy unspeakable and full of glory. God, through the death of His Son, had for ever relieved him of his burden. But before long he had to pass through the valley of the shadow of death where he was surrounded by darkness and by evil spirits who let loose dark floods of blasphemy upon his soul. In his *Grace Abounding to the Chief of Sinners* Bunyan tells us of his own deep conflicts and of his fear that his sins had risen beyond the pardoning mercy of God.

Heman the Ezrahite, who composed this Psalm, touched these depths also. Many a poor distressed soul has seen his own image in this mirror. God in His infinite wisdom and love has permitted that Heman's sorrows should be recorded in His Word that His afflicted people might know that some of His choicest saints had passed through conflicts and griefs as deep as, or deeper than their own.

A minister, preaching to a large congregation, once said that, like John Bunyan, some of God's people may sometimes fear that their sins have gone beyond God's forgiveness. 'But,' he continued, 'there are untold thousands singing before the throne in glory who have been through these same fears and tribulations.' Most of us sooner or later come to know 'the depths of Satan' and how grievous a thing sin is.

In one of his letters, John Newton makes the deeply impressive comment that one sure proof that such evil thoughts and fears often come through the temptations of the Adversary, and are contrary to our own will, is that, however deep our sorrow, our conscience is not involved. Heman's first words in the Psalm show how true is this remark. God was still his God. He was all his hope and salvation. God was, beyond all others, the Subject of his love and desire. Sin was a bitter grief to him because it shadowed the glory of the One whom he would have honoured by a life of holiness. There was still in his soul an holy boldness to pour out in prayer his contrite heart before the Brother born for adversity. If we sometimes find ourselves in these dark depths, let us remember that the first rays of that Sun which shall no more go down will soon change the shadow of death into morning.

In the light of eternity, man's life here is like the blink of the eye. In the Book of Genesis, we read of men who lived on this earth for hundreds of years, but the words 'and he died' follow the name of each one. 'We all do fade as a leaf.' Our life here is but a 'vapour that appeareth for a little time and then vanisheth away.' Generation after generation rises and falls before the face of Him who is from everlasting to everlasting. But beyond man's apparent nothingness is God's purpose for him. 'Man's chief end is to glorify God and to enjoy Him for ever.' For our fulfilment of that great end, God remembers how short our time is here. But do we? Another Psalm speaks of certain men whose 'inward thought is that their houses shall continue for ever and their dwelling places to all generations'.

A Christian minister once stood by a grave. When the coffin was lowered into the earth he asked a question. 'Who will be the last among us to descend into the grave?' To his question there was only silence. His own answer was: 'Oh, who but yourself?' Like the rich fool in the parable, we may speak of our future life in this world in terms of 'many years', while God may say, 'This night thy soul shall be required of thee'.

God's child would redeem his time. He would seek to make up for the years which he has wasted and spent in the service of the world and of sin, and with no thought of God. He would earnestly seek to put his house in order before the night comes when no man can work. God also would have us work in His vineyard and not stand idle all the day. The harvest is plenteous but the labourers are few. Our prayer should be: 'So teach us to number our days that we may apply our hearts unto wisdom.'

'Lord,' said Saul of Tarsus, 'what wilt Thou have me
do?' It was he who afterwards said, 'For me to live is
Christ'. For him to live was to preach Christ, to serve
Him, to suffer for Him and to bring souls into His fold.
Are we following his example?

PSALM 90: 'A TALE THAT IS TOLD'

This Psalm continues to speak to us of the fleeting and
transitory nature of life. In the original Hebrew, the
figure here used may be obscure; but we know that the
word 'tale' is expressive of its true meaning.

In primitive ages and societies the story teller was in
great demand. Into his stories he would often weave the
elements of love, of triumph, of surprise, and of tragedy.
Some stories would begin on a note of sorrow and end
on a note of joy. Others would end on the note of sorrow
only. Do we not all begin life's story on a note of tragedy?
We are all born in sin and shapen in iniquity. And the
longer we live, apart from the saving grace of God, the
deeper our predicament becomes. In the Old Testament
we read of many men whose life here ended with the
words: 'And he did that which was evil in the sight of
the Lord.' In a state of evil they came to the brink of
destruction and went over it. The day of their death
was worse than the day of their birth. Some might well
have ended their lives with the words once spoken by
King Saul: 'I have played the fool.' Judas Iscariot
ended his life with similar words: 'I have betrayed the

innocent blood.' And millions of the human race end the story of their lives in unspeakable tragedy.

Others there are whose lives tell a different tale. Such men are also mentioned in the Scriptures: 'And he did that which was right in the sight of the Lord.' Manasseh almost reached the brink of eternal woe, but his life ended, we believe, on a note of joy. He repented of his sin and returned to God 'while it was yet day'. The thief on the cross sought mercy and forgiveness within minutes of his death. How sweet a story he left behind him! His life ended on a note of everlasting joy.

In eternity we shall all have a story to tell. All the Lord's people will be found among the great multitude who stand 'without fault before the throne' singing, 'Unto Him who loved us and washed us from our sins in his own blood, and hath made us kings and priests unto God and his Father; to him be glory and dominion for ever and ever, Amen.'

### PSALM 91: 'SHIELD AND BUCKLER'

To those who are waging war with the powers of darkness and with sin, and who are conscious of the many perils to which they are exposed in this life, this Psalm is precious beyond words. God's people are heirs of God and of all His promises. They know that He can never go back on His Word. Their faith in His Word is one source of their comfort and the secret of their triumph over all their enemies. 'They overcame by the blood of the Lamb and by the word of their testimony.'

He, the omnipotent God, bestows the Word which becomes the testimony of His people. With such a support they can stand against all. Abraham knew this when he received the word, 'Fear not Abram, I am thy shield'. David overcame by the same faith when he carried the invisible 'sword of the Spirit' in going forth against the giant of Gath and the armies of the Philistines.

God may sometimes give us His word of promise when our skies are calm and when our enemies are not in sight. He gave His promise to Peter while he was still unaware of his danger. 'I have prayed for thee, that thy faith fail not.' The same promise was given to John Bunyan before Satan let loose his flood on his spirit. We knew of a man who, while still in a state of peace and quiet, was for several days aware that God was speaking to him and preparing him for dangers to come: 'The Lord hear thee in the day of trouble; the name of the God of Jacob defend thee.' Then came the storm; but God's Name and Word were his strong tower, his shield and buckler.

When Satan assailed the soul of the sinless Son of God with his blasphemous temptations, the written Word was His shield and sword – 'It is written . . . it is written . . . it is written'. Each of these was the fell stroke of His sword. We are told that after this threefold onslaught the devil departed from Him for a season. He went away to lick his wounds, the deep bruises from which he will never recover. We also shall overcome him, since his head is already bruised by Him who came to destroy his works: 'And the God of peace shall bruise Satan under your feet shortly.'

'The righteous shall flourish like the palm tree'

This lovely figure describes those who have experienced the miracle of spiritual transplantation. By nature we were all in the devil's garden, but out of that cold, poisonous and destructive environment, God graciously removes His people and plants them in His own house [or kingdom] where they flourish and bear fruit to His glory.

The palm tree is often found in dreary deserts. But there it flourishes, bearing a crop of rich and wholesome fruit. The secret of this lies in the fact that its roots are in touch with hidden springs or other sources of vitality. To the people of God, this world is a desert place. God's greatest saints, however, have often flourished in times and places of spiritual desolation. Enoch, Noah, Elijah, Daniel, and countless others in every age, flourished during barren days and in dry parched lands. But they were rooted and grounded in Christ, in His love, and in constant communion with Him. Their life was hid with Christ in God.

This also is the secret of their rectitude and tenacity. Many were the fierce storms which sought to uproot and break the righteous in other ages. What storms raged against Job, David, Paul and the martyrs and covenanters of other times! Young Margaret Wilson, for example, in the seventeenth century, faced the storm of cruel persecution and death, assured that she could not be separated from Christ and His love. Though a frail lily, she had, in the graces of the Spirit, the strong roots of a cedar tree.

The word 'righteous' [in the verse quoted above] means that these are a people who grow without the

crooked characteristics of a graceless world. 'Be ye
perfect even as your Father in heaven is perfect.'
Christ Himself is the supreme example of His people,
and although, unlike Him, they cannot be perfect in
this life, their daily prayer is:

> *Hold up my goings; Lord, me guide*
> *In those thy paths divine.*

One day 'we shall be like him, for we shall see him as
he is'.

Often the Lord's people cry, 'O my leanness, my
leanness'. They compare themselves with others of His
people, only to mourn over their poverty of soul. But
this is a healthy sign, and is the earnest of their promised
spiritual maturity in the courts of the Lord above. 'We
know not yet what we shall be.' We know, however,
what we desire to be – bearing fruit which shall be unto
holiness, and the end of which shall be everlasting life.

PSALMS 93-94: 'HOLINESS BECOMETH THINE HOUSE'

God dwells in the high and holy place, that is to say, in
that kingdom that is incorruptible and undefiled and
which fadeth not away. It is a place of eternal purity
and perfection. He has also His dwelling places in this
world, both within His Church and in the hearts of
His people. Of those with whom He dwells here He
demands holiness of life, and that He should be worshipped in sincerity of spirit and according to His
truth. 'Be ye holy for I am holy'.

When in our worship or conduct we deviate from
His Word, He forsakes us. Moses was commanded to
make and do all things according to the pattern which
He showed him on the Mount. When the sons of Aaron
deviated from His rule, they were destroyed. For the
same reason He turned His back upon His ancient
people and left them to perish in their folly. The holy
indignation with which our Lord, during His visit to
Jerusalem, swept God's house of all its abominations
was terrible to those whom He cast out. The place
dedicated to God's worship had become 'a den of
thieves' and 'the synagogue of Satan'. The 'throne of
iniquity' can have no fellowship with Him.

In our age there are thousands of so-called 'Christian'
Churches throughout the world whose doctrine and
mode of worship are utterly repulsive to God and to His
people. Once I visited a gracious woman of Christian
discernment. One Lord's day, at a holiday resort, she
went to a local church, filled to capacity. As she sat
there and listened to the minister she was grieved and
shocked at his spiritual ignorance. It took her days
before she got over a most disturbing experience. It
was not so with another lady whom I once met in
Edinburgh. She told me that she regularly attended a
well-known church in the city. 'And,' she said, 'I never
leave it without a good laugh.' In that same church,
and when the benediction was pronounced after the
evening service, the young gathered for their hour of
godless frivolity 'in the place below'. What an impassable
gulf lies between such places and the true Zion of God
where God desires to dwell!

Those who maintain a spiritual and scriptural

worship of God know that, in their own persons, they are the temple of the Holy Spirit. Christ dwells in their heart by faith. And they pray and long for the day when they shall be made perfect in holiness and eternally conformed to His holy will.

### PSALMS 95–100: THE EVER-ADORABLE GOD

The contents of these five Psalms are more or less identical. They are like the two previous Psalms, a call to praise and to worship God 'in the beauty of holiness'. They proclaim that from whatever viewpoint we think of God, He is infinitely desirable, glorious and worthy of our adoration. In all that He is, in all that He does, and in all that He permits, 'He is altogether lovely'. Every revelation He gives of Himself, whether in creation, providence or grace, strikes a chord of love and praise in the heart of His people. All His acts and works proceed from a nature which is holy and just and true. What provokes their sweetest song, however, is His communication of Himself, in indescribable love and goodness, to their souls. And they know that this is a blessing of endless duration. It eliminates time and sorrow: 'A thousand years with the Lord are as one day.' In His presence there is fullness of joy and at His right hand are pleasures for evermore. This ecstasy sometimes touches our heart here. We know that, united to Christ and in communion with God, this other world of joy and praise is already within our reach.

Is the irrational and inanimate creation, as God's immediate work, capable of praise? Yes. 'All thy works shall praise thee.' The millions of stars which move in their orbits have, we believe, their own song. In the Book of Genesis we are told that when God gave existence to the birds of the air and to the fish of the sea, He blessed them both. And, in their own way, they praise Him. Man, whom He created in His own image and likeness and for higher ends, could consciously adore Him as no other creature could. But when man sinned, disorder and rebellion took possession of his spirit and his song ceased.

The meaning of the Gospel is that God can recreate us and provide us with a new song, a sweeter and a nobler song than Adam could sing in a state of innocence. As redeemed men and women who have faith in Christ, this song is in our heart. Do we belong to those who can say:

> *O, for a thousand tongues to sing*
> *My great Redeemer's praise?*

### PSALM 101: 'WITHIN MY HOUSE'

Our home is the place where our faith and patience may often be tried. These domestic tensions need not be of a serious nature to upset us, and to produce reactions contrary to a true Christian spirit. To use an illustration, there are those who carry a box of wasps which they sometimes let loose in the family circle. There is the

harsh word, the temperamental explosion, or the sullen
silence. Disagreements on certain issues may arise to
disturb the peace which should prevail where the
Lord's presence is desired. Abraham, for example, had
to endure the domestic conflict between Sarah and
Hagar; but he sinned not with his mouth. The patience
linked with his faith enabled him to keep the door of
his lips. David was mocked by his wife in the hour of
his greatest spiritual joy; but Satan's fiery dart his
faith quenched. Abigail, the wife of a graceless churl,
endured her heavy cross throughout the years without
murmuring. Most of us, however, are not in this
category.

Men like Charles Simeon and the famous 'Fraser of
Brea' often grieved over their sullen dispositions and
quick tempers. They were holy men who often failed
to master wholly their besetting sin. John Wesley, on
the other hand, would utter no harsh word during
those hours of agony when his extremely possessive wife
would drag him by his hair around the room. A godly
Highland minister, who was married to a similar woman,
sat one day in his room reading his Bible. The door
opened and his wife entered. Her hand snatched the
Book from him and threw it into the fire. He looked
into her face and quietly made the remark: 'A warmer
fire I never sat at.' It was an answer that turned away
her wrath and marked the beginning of a new and
gracious life. His Jezebel became a Lydia. The thorn
became a lily.

Many find life in retrospect very distressing. One
day, a woman whom I had never seen before and have
never seen since, arrived at our door in Glasgow. Her

husband had died. In the silence and loneliness of her home she began to recall the occasional disagreements – on quite minor issues – between her and the loved one who was with her no more. In her deep distress we tried to comfort her. If we belong to the Lord, it is better far to forget the things which are behind, and to look forward to the day when perfect love and everlasting peace will unite us all together in the presence of Him against whom all our sins were really committed, but who will remember them no more.

### PSALM 102: THE MOURNFUL PRISONER

The experiences of this Psalm have often been those of God's people. Egypt became a veritable prison to Israel before God came to their rescue. Their groanings reached His ear and He came down to save them. Haman also had decreed their total destruction, but again God heard their prayers and freed them from the hand of the cruel enemy. On a subsequent occasion God raised up Cyrus that His people might be brought out of the bondage of Babylon.

All men are locked up in the prison house of sin, but the Son of God came to open the prison doors to those who are bound. He sends His Spirit into our hearts to convince us of our danger, plight and helplessness and to show us the only way of salvation and escape.

Some time ago I read the diary of a young man whom God had convinced of his lost condition. He came to realize that in the grasp of sin and in the hand of God's justice he was under sentence of death. But God heard his cry. In one hour he came to know 'the glorious liberty of the children of God'. The hills behind his native village would sometimes resound with his songs:

> *For my distressed soul from death*
> > *Delivered was by thee;*
> *Thou didst my mourning eyes from tears,*
> > *My feet from falling, free.*

This young man afterwards became a faithful ambassador of Christ, and he never wearied of telling all who came within the reach of his voice what God had done for his soul.

Although God's people, through the merits of Christ, are eternally set free from the power of sin, they are often brought into spiritual bondage. Christian and Hopeful were locked up in Doubting Castle by Giant Despair, till in their bosom they discovered the key of promise which unlocked the door and brought them again into God's path, to inhale once more the sweet air of Heaven and freedom. There is one place where God's people all meet. While in this tabernacle they groan, being burdened. The body of sin and death becomes heavier as they go on the way. The cry is often present with them: 'O wretched man that I am! Who shall deliver me from the body of this death?' How precious is the thought that although, at the end of our earthly pilgrimage, we enter the last river under this burden, when our feet shall touch the other side all our burdens shall have left us for ever. 'Sorrow and sighing shall flee away.'

Many of God's people are also bound with cords of pain and physical infirmities. I sometimes call on a choice jewel of Christ who has, through bodily ailment, for several years been confined to her bed and to her home. But she is quite resigned to drink the cup which the Lord has put into her hand. No word of murmuring ever escapes her lips. She knows that her light affliction is but for a moment.

But the words of our Psalm must be looked at on an eternal level. 'The sons of mortality' [as the Hebrew words of verse 20 may be translated] are to become the sons of everlasting life and deliverance, a state that shall be extended to their souls and bodies for ever. 'For if the Son shall make you free, ye shall be free indeed.' God's people are not to think of the grave as a prison house. In the grave their bodies are still united to Christ. There they sleep. There they rest. The keys of death are in the hand of their Lord. And when, at last, they awake they shall be satisfied in His likeness. 'We shall be like him, for we shall see him as he is.'

PSALM 103: THE RENEWAL OF LIFE
'Thy youth is renewed like the eagle's'

Naturalists tell us that, as a general rule, no bird lives longer than the eagle. Its life, however, is not one of continuous vitality. There are seasons when it moults, mopes and pines, and when its beak may become twisted and sensitive, so that it cannot hold its prey. It may also be located in places where there is little or nothing to sustain its life.

The Bible tells us of some of the saints who for a season pined away in bodily enfeeblement and spiritual discouragement, but whose lives God wonderfully renewed in answer to their prayers. Among them were Job, Heman, Hezekiah and David. The Gospels and the Apostolic age also provide us with many wonderful instances of those who, through the power of God, were raised from states of extreme weakness and even from the gates of death.

These words refer, in their highest meaning, to spiritual renewals. How often do our minds go back to the days of our spiritual youth! We remember the days when under the tree of life and in Christ's banqueting house our souls were filled with good things. The joy of the Lord was our strength. Now we may mourn over our leanness and over the years which the locusts have eaten. Like the prophet we may, figuratively speaking, pine away under our juniper tree. God, however, speaks to us as He spoke to him. 'Arise and eat, for the journey is too great for thee'; and he went for many days in the strength of the Lord's provision. Choice fare! His youth was renewed like the eagle's. We are commanded every day and every hour to come to the throne of grace that we may find grace to help us in time of need.

Do these words anticipate the day when we shall hunger no more, and when we shall soar on eagles' wings into a better world? Yes, they do. How impressive in this respect are the words of Dr Edward Payson who, on his death-bed and suffering indescribable pain, spoke to his friends about his deep joy in the Lord. 'I swim in a flood of joy which God pours down upon me, and I *know* that my happiness is but begun. It will last for ever . . . I am going to exist in an ocean of purity, benevolence and happiness to all eternity . . . God is now my All and in all . . . It seems as if my soul had found a pair of new wings and was so eager to try them that I would move out of this body to be for ever with the Lord.' Like some of God's people in their last hours, he knew that he was already soaring into the unfading dimensions of a happy eternity, to be 'with Christ which is far better'.

## PSALM 104: A SOLEMN PRAYER
### 'Let the sinners be consumed out of the earth'

If the former psalm speaks of God's grace, this psalm describes God's glory and mercy as revealed in the work of the creation and in the overrulings of His providence. The universe is like a majestic poem which declares the glory of the Lord. When God by the word of His power created all things He pronounced them 'very good'. It was then that the sons of God shouted for joy. How often are our hearts touched and our minds composed as we sit by the seaside or listen to the birds which warble in the trees! We look at the stars which grace the night sky, or at the sun as it sets over the distant hills. We say, 'O Lord our Lord, how excellent is thy name in all the earth'. The mystery of providence, whereby the needs of all His creatures are supplied by

His bountiful hand, also tells us that God's mercy is over all His works.

From such scenes and reflections we turn our eyes and minds to realize that while 'every prospect pleases, only man is vile'. History shows that man is utterly depraved. He has destroyed himself and brought disorder and moral chaos into God's world. God is long-suffering, but His purpose cannot be frustrated or His world permitted to continue for ever as it is. Hence the desire and the solemn plea of His servant: 'Let the sinners be consumed out of the earth, and let the wicked be no more.'

Two men who were on their way from a church once stood at the end of a street. On certain nights of the week the place where they had paused was the meeting-point of a number of the ungodly in that town. 'What is it,' the one asked the other, 'that often brings comfort to your mind in this day of rebuke and blasphemy?' 'It is,' said the other, 'the thought of the day when the wicked shall be subdued, and when the glory of the Lord shall cover the earth as the waters cover the sea.' Tears filled their eyes as they bade one another farewell and returned to their homes, to call on the name of the Lord, and plead that His will might be done on earth as it is in heaven.

## 'He sent a man before them'

The lives of many of the saints proclaim that the path to honour often lies through pain, sorrow and humiliation. It was so with the Lord, and it is so with many of His chosen servants. Those who are to partake of His glory in the world to come become partakers of His sufferings here. Like his Lord, the sufferings of Joseph began at home, for his own brethren did not believe in him. They hated him without a cause. They dismissed him as a mere dreamer of dreams. They afterwards became his potential murderers. It was in Egypt, however, that he passed through his greatest trial. A lewd woman sought to stain his good name and character. He was cast into prison. It is interesting to note that, as his sorrows began through his predictive dreams in his own family, his release and honour came through the solemn disclosures of God's providence in the same way. God's secret was with him. He told the baker of his doom, and Pharaoh's butler of his imminent restoration to his high office. He explained to Pharaoh the meaning of his mysterious night visions.

The purpose of the Lord in bringing His servant into so many afflictions was that he might be the means of preserving Jacob's family and, indeed, a multitude of other peoples throughout the years of famine. Egypt became the cradle in which the infant church found rest and nourishment for a season. Truly God's ways are in the deep. He 'moves in a mysterious way, his wonders to perform'.

'Remember me, O Lord, with the favour that thou bearest unto thy people'

God is a personal God, whether we come to know Him as our Redeemer, our Friend, or finally as our Judge. Sooner or later each of us must make a personal discovery either of His love or His wrath. Beside Christ on the cross hung two malefactors. The one man, in answer to prayer, made a glorious discovery of His love, while the other, nursing a resentment and blaspheming His Name, sank into perdition. 'Lord, remember me,' said the penitent one. There and then he was plucked as a brand from the burning. That day he was with Christ in paradise.

These words of our Psalm express a keen desire for the greatest 'favour' that God can bestow on sinful men and women. What, in a word, is this favour? Think first of what God removes from us. He forgives or puts away all our sins for ever. Once I listened to an old minister of Christ as before a meal he asked a blessing: 'Give us, O Lord, the blessing of blessings, the forgiveness of all our sins.' Think also of what God does. 'O visit me with thy salvation.' God can change us into new creatures. He who begins the good work in us will bring it to perfection. We shall at last stand in His presence without spot or wrinkle or any such thing. Above all, think of what He gives. Mary's portion will be the portion of all His people. 'The good part.' 'The Lord is my portion, saith my soul.' Temporal mercies and earthly ties fade away and are soon dissolved, but this 'favour' shall remain for ever. With it comes 'joy unspeakable and full of glory'. 'That I may rejoice in the gladness of thy nation.' I once visited a dear friend in the Lord who was dying. His lips were still moving and I could just hear his last faint whispers, 'Joy, joy, joy'. Then he was here no more.

'In thy presence is fullness of joy.'

### PSALM 107: THE LOVINGKINDNESS OF THE LORD

I still have vivid memories of an evening when I sat in a church in Stornoway listening to a remarkable sermon on this Psalm by Dr Martyn Lloyd-Jones of London. He dwelt on the different figures given in the Psalm which describe the peril and misery of man in a state of sin. All this, man had brought upon himself. 'Fools, because of their transgression and because of their iniquities, are afflicted.'

The Psalm speaks of men as living [or dying] in a wilderness of utter spiritual destitution. It is a place without water or bread. It is a land of darkness where men grope about like the blind. Men are also 'bound in affliction and iron' with no power to save themselves. They live in a world of recurring and ever-increasing storms [or wars] which no human effort can prevent. This, the preacher said, is a true picture of the world of today with all its boasted scientific and technological progress.

But God in His sovereign grace can change all this. He can make the wilderness to blossom as the rose and furnish our table with good things. Night He turns into day and He sets His captives free. Our restlessness gives way to a peace which passes all understanding. This is not a species of false optimism divorced from reality, but is, said the preacher, the uniform witness of the Christian Church and people in every age and place.

Beside me that evening sat an old friend, the Rev Duncan Morrison, then resident in Gairloch. After the service we shook hands and smiled. He had been deeply moved by the message, and especially by the unspeakable comfort which the words – 'so He bringeth them into their desired haven' – brought to his soul. And before long he was, like some others in that great audience, in that world where peace reigns through righteousness.

### PSALM 108: 'MINE, MINE, MINE'

When God gives His promise, its fulfilment is absolutely guaranteed. Nothing can disannul it, for it comes from the lips of Him who cannot lie. 'God hath spoken in His holiness.' His word is the expression of His changeless verity and perfection. And all His promises are confirmed by His oath. God gave all His promises to all His people within a covenant which, in Christ, is ordered in all things and sure. And since Christ has all power in heaven and in earth, no power can deprive them of their inheritance. Not even their own unbelief! 'If we believe not, yet he abideth faithful; he cannot deny himself.' Besides, like our persons, all His blessings are bought with a price. The death of Christ is an infallible guarantee that all whose names are in His

Book of Life shall, through faith and patience, inherit the promises. 'God who spared not his own Son, but delivered him up for us all, how shall he not with him also freely give us all things?' If we are the sons of God, then are we his heirs.

Before the true believer puts his hand on any one promise he must first embrace Christ Himself. Christ is mine, therefore all things worth having are mine in Him. The children of darkness, like the fool in the parable, may possess many temporal favours, but all these are mere husks which perish and leave them empty. They may say 'Health is mine; pleasure is mine; money is mine; a nice house is mine; and I have much goods laid up for many years'. But without Christ 'all is vanity and vexation of spirit'.

> *None else but Christ can satisfy.*
> *I have Christ; what want I more?*

While David rejoiced in God's promise with regard to the places and nations mentioned in this psalm, the well-spring of all his joy was in God Himself. This is what sanctifies and sweetens all our temporal favours.

How we ought to pray that God would increase our faith and give us a deeper assurance that He is ours in all His promises! for with this assurance would come a deeper joy!

A boy once went to ask his father for a certain gift. Then he rejoined his playmates, joyfully exclaiming, 'I got it, I got it!' 'And where is it?' they asked him. 'My father said I would get it,' was his answer, as he jumped his own height to the sky. And with God, likewise, His promise is as good as its fulfilment.

'God hath spoken, I will rejoice.' 'Christ is mine!' Unsearchable riches are mine! In Christ all God's promises are, 'Yea and Amen'.


PSALMS 109–110: 'THE RIGHT HAND'

In the first of these psalms we notice that Satan is spoken of as standing at the right hand of the evil man. Each serves the other. Satan uses his slaves to persecute those who carry the banner and bear the image of Christ in this world. But God shall at last clothe all the adversaries of His people with shame. He ever 'stands at the right hand of the poor'. Each of them may say with Asaph in another psalm, 'Thou hast holden me by my right hand'. As He is at their right hand they are at His. This honour is theirs through the Prince of Peace who is exalted at God's right hand. In Christ they also sit in the heavenly places.

*Upon thy right hand did the queen*
*In gold of Ophir stand.*

The right hand is a place of spiritual nearness. They are a people near to Him. 'The beloved of the Lord shall dwell in safety by Him.' It is a place of happiness. 'At thy right hand there are pleasures for ever more.'

How thankful we should be in these times, when the hearts of many are failing them for fear, that He to whom the Father has said, 'Sit Thou at my right hand' is going to exercise His power in the final overthrow of all His and our enemies, as well as in the uplifting of His own cause. 'The Lord at thy right hand shall strike through kings in the day of His wrath.' 'The wrath of the Lamb.' Out of the womb of a new spiritual morning millions of the human race, like the dew which falls from heaven, shall be made willing in the day of His power. A nation shall be born in a day. They shall be made willing to serve their only King. In that day a shout shall go up from the earth, the echoes of which shall resound through the confines of the whole universe, 'Alleluia: for the Lord God omnipotent reigneth'.

Throughout my ministerial life I have attended many sacramental services in a variety of places. To me, very often, the most solemn part of the service was the singing of the following words as we moved forward to the Lord's table to remember His death till He come:

> *In dwellings of the righteous*
> *Is heard the melody*
> *Of joy and health: the Lord's right hand*
> *Doth ever valiantly.*

> *The right hand of the mighty Lord*
> *Exalted is on high;*
> *The right hand of the mighty Lord*
> *Doth ever valiantly.*

PSALMS 111–112: THE POOR MAN'S FRIEND
'He hath dispersed, he hath given to the poor'

When a thief breaks into a house he does not always carry away everything that is of value; but when

Satan invaded the soul of man he removed all the choice gifts with which God had endowed him at his creation. Man lost communion with God and therefore all his spiritual riches.

But Christ came to 'restore that which He took not away'. God had endowed Him with unsearchable riches which, in infinite kindness, He was to disperse with both hands among millions of a lost race. At the great festal gathering in heaven people 'out of all nations and kindreds and people and tongues' will sit down with Him at His table to enjoy all the blessings of His purchased redemption. He is the heavenly Testator who in His last will and testament remembers the poor.

Behind all this – as the previous Psalm proclaims – lies His grace and compassion. 'The Lord is gracious and full of compassion.' And all these spiritual riches His people will never lose, for they are secure within a 'righteousness which endureth for ever.'

The Lord Jesus tells us that it is more blessed to give than to receive. One of the joys set before Him was that which He would have in forgiving men their sins and in blessing them with a life which shall never end. Some of His people have in a minor way tasted of this joy themselves. The joy of giving to the poor!

In a certain congregation, for example, there was once a good man of considerable wealth. He spent little on himself or on his own comfort. Towards the end of each year he would write out a sheaf of cheques which he sent under the name of 'A Friend' to many worthy and needy causes. And the cause of Christ, both at home and abroad, had priority in his heart over all others.

The excellent C. T. Studd inherited a large fortune which he gave away in one hour to help those who were seeking to advance the kingdom of Christ in England. 'This was no fool's plunge on his part. It was his public testimony before God and man that he believed God's Word to be the surest thing on earth, and that the hundredfold interest which God has promised in this life, not to speak of the next, is an actual reality for those who believe it and act on it.' Invested in the bank of heaven, it was both safe and yielded good interest.

There are, however, many who make a profession of religion and who, though they have plenty to give, do not follow in the footsteps of their Lord or of these two worthy men.

### PSALM 113: THE HAPPY MOTHER

'He maketh the barren woman to keep house, and to be a joyful mother of children'

A typical oriental woman knows no greater humiliation than, in a state of wedlock, to remain childless. Instances of this are found in the Bible in the lives of such women as Sarah, Rachel, Hannah and Elisabeth. But their sorrow God turned into joy by blessing them with sons who became His witnesses in their own day.

The words we quote are both typical and prophetic. For thousands of years the Gentile world knew nothing of God's grace, but God's Word anticipated the day when multitudes out of the Gentile nations would find their way into the bosom of the Church to make her a joyful mother of children. 'And the Gentiles shall come to thy light, and kings to the brightness of thy rising.' 'Who are these that fly as a cloud and as doves to their windows?' God transferred His presence and saving power from Israel to other peoples, and because of their unbelief, He left Israel desolate, though not entirely so.

Spiritually speaking, His Israel is today like a barren woman. But God is going to enlarge and bless her again. He is still espoused to her in His covenant promise. 'The children whom thou shalt have after thou hast lost the other, shall say again in thine ears, The place is too strait for me . . . Then shalt thou say in thine heart, Who hath begotten me these? . . . Behold I was left alone; these, where had they been?' Happy day for them and for us too!

Apart from our own salvation, perhaps there is no joy in the Christian life comparable to that of bringing souls to Christ and into His Church. A faithful servant of the Lord, at the beginning of his ministry, was once informed that he had been the means of leading a certain person to Christ. For a moment he was silent. Then he quietly said: 'Suffer now thy servant to depart in peace, for mine eyes have seen thy salvation.'

Some years ago I visited and preached in a certain congregation. The minister in whose manse I stayed was blessed with a family of four sons who came to the Lord in their early years. On the Sabbath afternoon they went into a room by themselves. Then we heard the singing:

*Behold, how good a thing it is, and how becoming well,*
*Together such as brethren are, in unity to dwell!*

Their mother's face radiated joy as their voices reached her ear. They had been the subjects of her prayers from the day they were born.

God's Word reminds us that, as the natural birth is preceded by travail, so it is in the spiritual realm. 'He shall see of the travail of His soul and shall be satisfied.' 'As soon as Zion travailed she brought forth her children.' It was Paul who said: 'My little children, of whom I travail in birth again until Christ be formed in you . . .' Is this our exercise of soul in our own day?

### PSALMS 114–115: HELP AND SHIELD
#### 'He is their help and their shield'

The implication of these reassuring words is that the Church of God is always subject to danger. God, however, is ever round about her as a wall of fire. When Israel was passing through the Red Sea He was a light and shield to them while, in the same hour, He was darkness and destruction to Pharaoh and his hosts.

These words are thrice repeated in the one hundred and fifteenth Psalm. There is a trinity of evil at work around us – the world, the flesh, and the devil; but confronted with the all-powerful Triune God – the shield of His people – they are already defeated. Christ overcame them, and 'because I overcame, ye shall overcome also'.

These thrice-repeated words may remind us that our exalted King exercises a threefold office on behalf of His people. He is their Prophet, Priest and King. No fiery dart from the bow of the adversary ever pierced through this shield. And Christ's offices are linked in a threefold promise: 'Fear thou not, for I am with thee; be not dismayed for I am thy God; I will *strengthen* thee; yea, I will *help* thee; yea, I will *uphold* thee with the right hand of my righteousness.'

There are also three classes of people mentioned in the psalm. These are – 'Israel', 'The house of Aaron' and those 'that fear the Lord'. Whatever office we exercise in His Church, or whoever we are, His protecting care is extended to every member of His flock. No one can pluck them out of His hand.

We notice also the threefold exhortation which precedes these words – 'Trust in the Lord'. These words remind us of the peril of idolatry against which the Psalm specially warns us, as also does the New Testament in such words as 'Little children, keep yourselves from idols'. Not that we worship wood and stone, but we may, in a subtle and even unconscious way, give undue place to the creature, to self-exaltation, or set our affections upon mere 'things'. An older generation of Christians would sometimes speak of their struggle to subdue 'Mr Self', who, if he could, would set himself on a pedestal within their souls. And in an age of material comfort we should beware lest the things which we possess bring us into a state of spiritual destitution. Trust in the Lord and in no other.

'Precious in the sight of the Lord is the death of his saints'

These words are 'precious' not only when we relate them to the death of God's people, but also and especially to the death of our Lord. It was through His death that death was destroyed, sin removed, Satan vanquished and the grave robbed of its prey. It is through the shedding of His precious blood that we are accounted righteous before God. To all who believe He is precious, for they know that if He had not died they would have for ever remained alienated from God. The death of His saints is precious to God because He loved them in the One who died for them.

'Saint' is a familiar word in our age. The Roman Church, for example, put certain types of men and women on high pedestals to be worshipped or admired as 'saints'. In the context of God's Word, however, all true believers are saints. They are God's workmanship and not man's. They are new creatures in Christ, and vessels unto honour. Their reconciliation through His blood, their regeneration and sanctification of the Holy Spirit, and their loving obedience to God in His Word, give them this title and privilege. Nothing else does.

What makes the death of His people so precious to God? Is it not the fact that their death is not real death, but real life? What happens when we die? Our souls immediately pass into God's presence. Our bodies rest in the grave till the resurrection. 'If a man believe in me', said Christ, 'though he were dead yet shall he live,' and 'I will raise him up at the last day'. Our death marks our eternal and final deliverance from all sin. It marks our rest from all toil, labour and sufferings. 'Go thou thy way till the end be; for thou shalt rest,

and stand in thy lot at the end of the days.' Then shall
all our spiritual hopes be realized. Then shall we see
the face of our Beloved. Our death will also mark our
safe arrival in our eternal home. The bride is at home,
to be for ever with her Lord.

> *'Midst the light, and peace, and glory*
> *Of the Father's home,*
> *Christ for me is waiting, watching,*
> *Waiting till I come.*
>
> *There, amidst the love and glory,*
> *He is waiting yet;*
> *On His hands a name is graven*
> *He can ne'er forget.*
>
> *There amidst the songs of heaven,*
> *Sweeter to His ear*
> *Is the footfall through the desert*
> *Ever drawing near.*
>
> *He and I, in that bright glory,*
> *One deep joy shall share;*
> *Mine, to be for ever with Him,*
> *His, that I am there.*

[Paul Gerhardt]

A friend once told me of a visit he made to a city
hospital to see a godly young woman who was very ill.
The congregation to which she belonged had been
praying for her recovery. 'Tell them,' she said, 'not to
pray for my recovery.' She made it clear that she was
ready to depart and to be with Christ which is far
better.

When we stand at the bedside of our loved ones who die in the Lord, we cannot but mourn. But we sorrow not as those who have no hope. We shall meet again in the presence of Him who is the bright and morning Star, and to whom the ingathering of all His saints shall be.

### PSALMS 117–118: THE HEAD CORNER STONE

The traditional and possibly true story of how, in the building of the second Temple, the stone which had been prepared as the head corner stone was, before its final setting in the building, repeatedly rejected by the builders, might be the literal background of the verse, 'The stone which the builders refused is become the head stone of the corner'. These words, however, are typical of Him who was in the world in the likeness of sinful flesh. God had foreordained Him to be the only foundation and Head of His Church, but He was rejected by 'the builders', that is, the religious leaders of His own nation. They were looking for a Messiah who would appear in outward splendour, to exalt the nation and subdue all its political enemies. But Him who was despised and rejected of men, God highly exalted and gave a name which is above every name. In the estimation of all His people also, both in heaven and on earth, Christ is the 'First and the Last'.

In the building of God's spiritual temple, Christ, the chief corner stone, unites both Jews and Gentiles. All the living stones in this temple are laid by His hands,

and, in their final perfection shall be brought forth
with shoutings of 'Grace, grace, unto it'. 'This is the
Lord's doing; it is marvellous in our eyes.'

Many of God's choice servants have passed through
this same process of rejection and humiliation. For
example, Jesse's sons, because of their impressive
physical appearance, were put before David. But
David was God's choice. Even his own father had
almost forgotten he existed when Samuel was sent to
anoint him as king. Within the visible Church some
aspirants to office, because of their 'airs' and gestures,
have been chosen to occupy important spheres of
labour while abler and better men have been passed
by. Paul, the greatest man who ever graced God's
Church on earth, was despised by some of his own
contemporaries. To them 'his bodily presence was weak
and his speech contemptible'. But he was the Lord's
chosen vessel to bear His name before 'the Gentiles,
and kings, and the children of Israel'.

Men like Jonathan Edwards, Thomas Boston and
Lachlan Mackenzie were in their day ignored by proud
men of ecclesiastical influence, who tried to seal their
lips. But by their spoken and written words they stand
out in retrospect, and in the estimation of God's people,
as among the brightest stars of their age. 'The first
shall be last, and the last first.' It is God 'who hath
put down the mighty from their seats and exalted
them of low degree'.

'O how love I thy law!'

This Psalm is made up of what some have appropriately called the Golden Alphabet of the Bible. By God's law, so often spoken of in this song, the Psalmist means that every syllable from the lips of God commanded his affection. 'His mouth', said the Church, 'is most sweet.' The Bible, from beginning to end, is the perfect revelation of God's will. 'Every word of God is pure.' Those who wrote the Scriptures did so as they were moved by the Holy Spirit. The great original 'is for ever settled in Heaven' within the mind of God. It shall never, therefore, pass away. To all who love God, the Bible is the voice of their beloved and eternal King.

The law, or the Word of God, is not merely written in a book: it is also engraven on His people's heart. It is their guide through this dark world. 'Thou shalt hear a word behind thee saying, This is the way, walk ye in it.' It is their spiritual nourishment, 'Thy words were found and I did eat them.' 'How sweet are Thy words unto my taste! Yea, sweeter than honey to my mouth!' It is their support in every trial. 'Remember the word unto thy servant upon which thou hast caused me to hope.' 'This is my comfort in my affliction.' It is their source of joy and the substance of their song. 'I rejoice at thy word, as one that findeth great spoil.' 'Thy statutes have been my songs in the house of my pilgrimage.' It is, above all, the pure mirror in which they behold the glory of the Lord and whereby they are 'changed into the same image from glory to glory, even as by the Spirit of the Lord'. It is also the sword of the Spirit by which they are to overcome all their enemies. 'His truth shall be thy shield and buckler.'

And because the theme is inexhaustible, we can only exclaim with David, 'O how love I thy law'.

One evidence of our love to God's law is that it is our meditation in this life, and that evil men's opposition to it fills us with grief. 'Rivers of waters run down mine eyes, because they keep not thy law.' A few years ago I read the private memoir of a good woman. Here and there she mentioned her nights of weeping over the desecration of God's law and especially of His holy Sabbath Day.

Some of God's saints have tried to express their undying love to God's Word both in their life and death. Edward Payson directed that, while lying in his coffin, a label should be attached to his breast which all those to whom he had preached the Gospel might see before he lay in his grave. 'Remember the words which I spake unto you while I was yet present with you.' And was it not the excellent Bishop Ryle who commanded that his old Bible should lie on his heart in the grave? 'O how love I thy law.' This is a love, we believe, that will continue to deepen within our beings for ever.

PSALMS 120–121: BITTER AND SWEET
'Woe is me.' 'The Lord thee keeps'

These two Psalms express both the trial and the faith of God's child. In the one we find David surrounded by many sharp thorns, while in the other his eye is upon the Lord who keeps him night and day. But he knows that, however deep his afflictions, God in His care of him will never leave him.

The note of sorrow in the first Psalm was due to the painful environment in which the Psalmist found himself. 'Woe is me, that I sojourn in Mesech, that I dwell in the tents of Kedar.' His cruel neighbours hated him without cause. In such situations we find many of God's saints in the past. In Sodom the soul of Lot was vexed by the behaviour of the wicked. When Abraham entered Gerar he knew 'that the fear of God was not in this place', and that for the sake of Sarah his wife the wicked would have no scruples in taking his life.

John Calvin speaks of God's hidden ones in Europe during the age of Papal darkness. 'For these', he wrote, 'who have any feeling of true piety within them, it will be impossible to be in the midst of those pollutions [of the Church of Rome] without great anguish of spirit.'

Many of us in this age find ourselves in similar situations. The wicked walk on all sides. People live in fear of the savage, lawless type who prowl in the night in so many of our communities. Others, while living among a well-behaved people, find but few with whom they can have any Christian fellowship.

A few years ago I called to see a friend who mourned over the departure of those friends in the Lord whose fellowship she had enjoyed in other days; but a sweet drop in her cup was the good hope that in a little while she would rejoin them where the wicked cease from troubling and where loneliness is unknown.

But the Psalmist knew where to go in his trials and loneliness, and in whom he should trust. The Shepherd of Israel, he knew, was ever beside him. No slumber ever touches His eyes. All the saints are in His hand. They are kept by His power both in their coming in and in their going out. Over them is the pillar of cloud by day and the pillar of fire by night.

A famous Christian lady missionary – Mildred Cable – tells the story of the song to which she and her friends listened on a certain night as they were surrounded by bands of savage men. The song, they believed, was sung by those ministering spirits who constantly watch over all the heirs of salvation:

> *Thy foot he'll not let slide nor will*
> *He slumber that thee keeps.*
> *Behold, he that keeps Israel,*
> *He slumbers not nor sleeps.*
>
> *The Lord shall keep thy soul, he shall*
> *Preserve thee from all ill.*
> *Henceforth thy going out and in*
> *God keep for ever will.*

### PSALM 122: THE BELOVED CITY
'Pray for the peace of Jerusalem'

This lovely Psalm expresses the joy, the prayer, and longings which dwell in the heart of those who desire a better country and that city which God has prepared for them.

There were occasions in Israel, such as the annual feast of the passover, which commanded the interest of the tribes, which were associated with great events and which also expressed the power and love of Jehovah toward His people. On such occasions many from every part of the land might be seen moving toward Jerusalem, 'the city of the Great King'. Prayer and praise arose from many hearts as the beloved city came into view. Their prayers would be for the peace and prosperity of Zion, while the well-spring of the true Israelites' joy was their fellowship with God and with one another in Him.

During the great evangelical revival of the eighteenth century in England, Wales and Scotland, this Psalm had a unique place in the affections of the great multitudes who gathered in their different communities to worship God. During sacramental occasions in the Scottish Highlands, for example, bands of men and women could be seen walking long distances to hear the Gospel. Prayer, praise and Christian conversation were their spiritual exercises on the way. And on the Monday, after the services of the week had come to an end, these words could be heard in many homes where ministers and people met to bid one another a fond, but not a final, farewell.

> *Pray that Jerusalem may have*
>   *Peace and felicity:*
> *Let them that love thee and thy peace*
>   *Have still prosperity.*
>
> *Now, for my friends' and brethren's sakes,*
>   *Peace be in thee, I'll say.*
> *And for the house of God our Lord,*
>   *I'll seek thy good alway.*

They hoped and believed that in the Jerusalem which is above, they would all meet to go no more out. One great evidence of our being in the way to that glorious city is that there is nothing in this world that commands our concern or interest more than the prosperity of God's Zion and of all those who seek its good in every part of the world.

## PSALMS 123–124: THE BROKEN SNARE
### 'The snare is broken'

God's eye is not on His people only; Satan and all his snares are under His eye as well. To us these snares may often be invisible and seemingly innocuous; but He knows all the dangers which lie in our path.

Even in our unconverted days, when we were blind and foolish, God often kept us from many of the paths 'wherein destroyers go'. That great man of God, Archie Cook, used to tell the story of the night when, as a young man, he was present at a dance. God's Spirit had been striving with him, but he would stifle the warnings which so often reached his conscience. And there he was, having his fling among the ungodly. What happened in that hour he could never explain. He saw himself on the brink of woe. The vision was so devastating and so real that they had to carry him out of the place. God broke the snare and rescued his soul. He became a preacher of the Gospel, and was the means of bringing many souls to Christ in his day. He never preached a sermon without warning the careless and the ungodly that the way of transgressors is hard, and that, without repentance, it leads to eternal death.

Another eminent man of God, J. Anderson, who laboured for Christ in Canada, often told of the night when his father stood in his way and ordered him to his bed! He too was 'all set' for a night of frivolity with the ungodly. In bed, where he wept his eyes dry, he felt that his father was cruel and most uncharitable. But in after days, often did he bow his knee in prayer to thank God for a parent who cared for his soul, and who kept him out of one of Satan's snares.

In her lovely book, *My Beloved*, Cathie MacRae tells a similar story of her gracious mother's warning – 'that her blood was now on her own head' – when she was prepared to join her companions in the dance hall.

All these had a wonderful story to tell of God's love in bringing them out of the way of moral and spiritual danger into the way of safety and everlasting happiness.

These words, however, are also applicable to the Church of Christ in this world, and to those who are already in a state of grace. The snares which Satan lays in the path of God's people are too many to be mentioned. The snare is often our own besetting sin – 'the sin that doth so easily beset us'. But 'hitherto hath the Lord helped us'. 'The snare is broken and we are escaped.' 'I have escaped,' said Job, 'by the skin of my teeth.' But one day soon we shall be for ever beyond the reach of all those who would destroy us.

Meantime, and in the words of an earlier Psalm, may we continue to look to the Lord until His mercy is crowned with victory.

> *Let God's redeemed say so, whom he*
> *From th' enemy's hand did free.*

### PSALMS 125-126: TEARS BEFORE JOY
'They that sow in tears shall reap in joy'

One can imagine the anguish of the poor eastern peasant as, in the spring of the year, he goes forth with his large lapful of corn and scatters it over his piece of prepared soil. His family need the grain for their daily bread, but unless some of it is sown they cannot live. If the present hour, however, is one of anxiety, the time of harvest is one of joy. The precious seed has brought forth sixty or an hundredfold.

The spiritual significance of these words, however, rises infinitely higher than their literal setting. Where do we begin? We begin with the Man Christ Jesus. There never was any sorrow like His sorrow. In the garden of Gethsemane 'His sweat was, as it were, great drops of blood falling down to the ground'. A cup was put into His hand which contained all the agonies and sorrows which His people would otherwise have to endure for ever. But if His tears betokened unspeakable sorrow, His joy shall be matchless. 'He shall see of the travail of His soul and shall be satisfied.' For the joy set before Him He endured the cross and despised the shame. Through

[179]

His sufferings and death, a great multitude which no man can number shall rejoice for ever in His presence.

Within the Church of Christ in this world 'those who are winners of souls are often weepers for souls'. The Church, which is Christ's spouse, is spoken of in the Scriptures as a woman travailing in birth for her spiritual seed. What a harvest would be reaped if all who profess the name of Christ obeyed His command: 'The harvest truly is plenteous, but the labourers are few; pray ye therefore the Lord of the harvest, that He will send forth labourers into His harvest.'

Many years ago a woman stood at the door of her cottage, her face beaming with joy. Passing her door were men and women on their way to the local Prayer Meeting. For many days she had been wrestling with God for a day of His power. Now He had 'come down like rain upon the mown grass: as showers that water the earth'. The spiritual wilderness by which she had been surrounded hitherto was beginning to blossom as the rose.

Let us think, for a moment, of God's command to us. 'Cast thy bread upon the waters, for thou shalt find it after many days.' 'In the morning sow thy seed, and in the evening withhold not thine hand; for thou knowest not whether shall prosper, either this or that, or whether they both shall be alike good.' Let us think also of His promise, 'For in due season we shall reap if we faint not'. Only in eternity shall many of the Lord's people come to know that their 'labour is not in vain in the Lord'.

The history of the Church is replete with instances of saints who felt discouraged as they tried to do something for the Lord. Some of his friends, to whom John Bunyan had showed the substance of his immortal dream, advised him to put it for ever out of sight. But God led him to sow the precious seed which has proved and will yet prove a source of blessing to countless souls till the end of time. In a smaller way, those whose tears and sowings are perhaps unknown to all but God shall in no wise lose their reward. Their tears are treasured in His bottle, and in the glorious world above, God will yet acknowledge their labour of love.

### PSALMS 127–128: THE HAPPY HOME

A law was observed in Israel with regard to the first-born son. He was dedicated to the Lord, and given to Him as His heritage. All Christian parents should pray that their children should, by His grace, become the Lord's. Happy will those be who, in the world to come, shall be able to say, 'Behold I and the children whom God hath given me'. In their Christian duties many parents are remiss. We know of homes which profess to be Christian where parents conduct family worship and retire to bed while their children are often absent. Where are they? In companies and in places where their souls are in jeopardy. There are parents who on the Lord's Day sit in the church pew with their family absent. Such neglect often paves the way for domestic anxiety and grief. The Lord will not dishonour His promise: 'Train up a child in the way he should go: and when he is old he will not depart from it.'

The homes depicted in these Psalms are happy because the parents fear the Lord and walk in His way. The head of the home labours for the welfare of his family. His wife is as a fruitful vine; her hands are diligent and her manners are gracious. To the end of their days John and Charles Wesley could trace their interest in the things of God to the influence and prayers of their excellent mother. Very often it is the wife or mother who makes the home happy and who exercises the greater influence on the children. In the Old Testament we read of many a king who 'did evil in the sight of the Lord'. Then come the ominous words, 'And his mother's name was . . .'

The emblem used in the Psalm to describe the children of God-fearing parents is truly delightful. 'Thy children like olive plants round about thy table.' Dr W. M. Thomson, in his famous work, *The Land and the Book*, explains this passage. 'Follow me,' he writes, 'into the grove . . . The aged and decayed olive tree is surrounded by several young and thrifty shoots which spring from the root of the venerable parent. They seem to uphold, protect and embrace it. We may even fancy that they now bear that load of fruit which would otherwise be demanded of the feeble parent. Thus do good and affectionate children gather round the table of the righteous. Each contributes something to the welfare of the whole – a beautiful sight with which may God refresh the eyes of every friend of mine.'

Yes! we have sometimes seen, with our own eyes, aged and disabled parents surrounded by a devoted and affectionate family. There they stand, tenderly ministering to the father or the mother, even in their last moments, who had brought them up in the fear of the Lord and who had led them into God's garden to enjoy unfading life.

### PSALMS 129–131: 'TILL THE DAY DAWN'

'My soul waiteth for the Lord, more than they that watch for the morning'

These three Psalms give us an impressive picture both of the sufferings and the soul exercise of God's people in this troubled life. There are sufferings which come from men, and there are sufferings which come from invisible sources, or from inward trials. David's own life is an illustration of this; so too is Paul's and the lives of countless numbers of God's people in every age.

Abel, the first man who bore the image of Christ in this world, was persecuted and murdered by Cain, his brother. David was surrounded for many days by cruel men who would have torn his life asunder. Paul gives us an appalling catalogue of the physical sufferings which he had to endure at the hands of evil men. Over many years in Europe the papal anti-Christ opened numberless graves into which he threw the charred or mangled bodies of those who would not assume his blasphemous image. 'And in her was found the blood of prophets and of saints and of all that were slain upon the earth.' These words coincide with the witness of the Church. 'Many a time have they afflicted me from my youth, may Israel now say: The plowers plowed upon

[183]

my back: they made long their furrows.' 'For Thy sake are we killed all the day long; we are counted as sheep for the slaughter.'

It often happens that in our physical sufferings our joy in the Lord remains with us. A minister of Christ who has only recently passed through indescribable agonies under the cruel hand of Russian Communism remarks that his greatest joys were related to his greatest pains. This was the Lord's doing. His presence changed his dungeon into a little heaven. Edward Payson remarked on his death-bed: 'I have suffered twenty times as much as I could in being burnt at the stake, while my joy in God so abounded as to render my sufferings not only tolerable, but welcome. Were the whole world trying to minister to my comfort, they could not add one drop to my cup of happiness.'

But it is not always so. John Owen, in his great treatise on Psalm 130, speaks of 'the depths' into which the Lord permits many of His people to come. In the Christian life there are sometimes depths of spiritual depression which almost border on despair. Job, Asaph, and Heman, Bunyan and Cowper, had their seasons of darkness, the terror of which they could not easily describe. Giant Despair is not unknown to many of God's choice saints. A Christian lady once asked me about a minister of Christ to whom she was led to apply these words, 'Thou hast showed Thy people hard things: Thou hast made us to drink the wine of astonishment.' At that time, as I knew, this good man was passing through great inward trials.

But 'the morning cometh'. 'My soul waiteth for the Lord more than they that watch for the morning: I

say, more than they that watch for the morning.'
'But unto you that fear my name shall the Sun of
righteousness arise with healing in his wings.' The deeper
our sorrows here, the sweeter our joys shall be where
our Sun shall no more go down. 'Now ye have sorrow;
but I will see you again and your heart shall rejoice, and
your joy no man taketh from you.'

As we see in the last of these Psalms there are two
graces which thrive under the chastening hand of the
Lord. The one is humility; the other is quiet resignation. 'My heart is not haughty, nor mine eyes lofty.'
'I have quieted myself, even as a weaned child.' 'Thou
wilt keep him in perfect peace whose mind is stayed on
thee, because he trusteth in thee.'

### PSALM 132: GOD'S PLACE OF REST

There is no place but where God is. In the words of
Pascal, 'His centre is everywhere; His circumference is
nowhere.' But there are three places in which He dwells
in a peculiar, intimate and loving manner, places where
His love and presence are enjoyed. He dwells in Heaven,
which is the saints' everlasting Home. There we shall
for ever rest in His love, and He will rest in ours. He
dwells within the visible Church on earth. Over a long
period of time He dwelt in Zion, among Israel His
people. The symbols, or evidences, of His presence
among them were visible in the pillar of fire by night and
of cloud by day and invisible in the Holy of Holies. But
because of their many transgressions, God removed His

candlestick from their midst and set it in other places where spiritual darkness had hitherto prevailed. This removal of His glory, or presence, is by far the greatest judgment that He may bring upon us in this world.

We know of places which, over a hundred years ago, could be described as 'Bethels', but which are now in a state of spiritual desolation. In such places God once had a people who would plead with Him not to become a stranger in the land. In a certain Scottish village, for example, there was a company of men and women who, if they felt that something among them had grieved the Spirit of the Lord, would spend hours together in prayer. And as long as they were on the scene the Lord dwelt among them. Not far from where these people lived, a minister of Christ would 'prevent the dawning of the day', wrestling with the Lord that His presence might still tarry among them. And before he died God blessed that place with a day of His power, and many souls came to know the Lord.

The third place where the Lord desires to dwell is in the hearts of His people. They are the temple of the Holy Spirit. Christ dwells in their heart by faith. The Church in the Song of Solomon would not have the daughters of Jerusalem disturb her Beloved as long as He was willing to stay with her.

Many years ago in the parish of Resolis a devoted minister of Christ, Hector MacPhail, spoke of one evidence of Christ being present in the hearts of His people. He made a comment on the words of Job, 'O that I knew where I might find him!' 'Where,' he asked, 'shall he find God for Job?' He answered 'We may find Him in the living desire within his soul after Him.'

David longed for the day when, without sin or sorrow, he would dwell with Him for whom his soul thirsted:

> *My soul for God, the living God,*
> *Doth thirst: when shall I near*
> *Unto thy countenance approach,*
> *And in God's sight appear?*

And what was God's answer?

'This is my rest for ever: here will I dwell; for I have desired it.' 'Blessed are they who hunger and thirst after righteousness, for they shall be filled.'

### PSALMS 133–134: 'THE DEW OF HERMON'

Christ was anointed with the precious ointment of the Holy Spirit into a threefold office. He is Prophet, Priest and King. And this anointing did not rest, exclusively, on Himself. It went down to the skirts of His garments. It extends, in other words, to the whole of His mystical Body, the Church of the First-born. 'But ye have an unction from the Holy One, and ye know all things.'

He has also the dew of His youth, which rests on every lily in His garden, both in this lower vale and in the Sharon of glory. In Hosea God gives His promise to His people: 'I will be as the dew unto Israel: he shall grow as the lily, and cast forth his roots as Lebanon.' God's Israel grows in grace and in the knowledge of Christ. The Church in the Song could describe her Beloved in a way that others could not. In every part of

His Person He was 'altogether lovely'. 'The Lily of the valleys' was, by far, the fairest Flower in her garden. It was from Him that all the other 'plantings of the Lord' in the garden derive their life and beauty. They all grow in His likeness. They are, by the dew of His grace, and by His Spirit, 'changed into the same image'.

True believers grow also in humility. The more the lily receives of the dew the more it bows its head. Under the weight of His blessing God's children are clothed with humility. In the world above, under 'an exceeding weight of glory', our holy humility shall remain with us for ever and ever.

The fragrance of holiness should also be present in our lives. Once I travelled on a train where an old man and a younger friend spoke together of 'the things which concern the King'. At the end of the journey, and as the young man was putting on his coat, the other quoted the words of the Psalm:

> *Of aloes, myrrh, and cassia,*
> *A smell thy garments had.*

In this world those who know the Lord shall have tribulation. The words, 'As the lily among thorns, so is my love among the daughters' describe God's people here. But the day is coming when 'there shall be no more pain', and when all the thorns and briars which distressed them here shall be no more. Paul has no longer the thorn in his flesh. He is but one of the great multitude 'who came out of great tribulation'.

The fruit of this blessing is precious beyond words. It brings with it harmony and peace. A few years ago a minister preached in a congregation which had been much disturbed and disunited by the great adversary. As the preacher gave out the closing Psalm, heads were bowed and tears began to flow from many eyes.

> *Behold, how good a thing it is,*
> *And how becoming well,*
> *Together such as brethren are*
> *In unity to dwell!*

The next Psalm reminds us that all whom God so blesses, bless Him. The spiritual instinct of the gracious soul is to bless God.

> *For there the blessing God commands,*
> *Life that shall never end.*

## PSALMS 135–137: 'THE GLORY OF THE LORD'

These Psalms present us with a fourfold view of God. He is before us as the Creator of all things. These He brought into being by 'the word of His power' and 'according to the good pleasure of His will'. 'For that thy name is near thy wondrous works declare.' The universe is one evidence of His eternal power and Godhead. 'Without him [Christ] was not anything made that was made.' Do we see Him in His work of Creation? Many years ago, while I was still a young man, I travelled over to the Island of Skye on a boat. The night was cloudless, pleasant and calm. The orbs of heaven seemed to smile down on the distant Coolin hills! The worthy old man who stood beside me was quite entranced by the scene. 'In all these,' he softly remarked, 'we see the finger of God.'

The Creator is also the sustainer of all His creatures. In Christ 'all things are held together'. All His creatures are wholly dependent on Him for their existence and continuance. 'The eyes of all wait upon thee; and thou givest them their meat in due season.' Do we see this in His providential kindness toward us from day to day? Our daily bread comes from that blessed hand which bears the print of the nails.

Long ago in a certain town in Germany a good Christian woman was one night sitting by her dying fire. Her children were beside her weeping, for there was nothing for them in the home to eat. The mother kept assuring them that the Lord would provide for their needs as He had promised. At that point one of the little girls said to her mother, 'Look, mother, at the coin in the side of the peat.' The mother looked, and pulled the coin out from the bosom of the burning ember. In the morning she was told that the coin was of much value. That day, as she laid her table and filled her cupboards with good things, they could not but praise 'The Giver of all good'.

Our sustainer is also our preserver. He is the Captain of the host of the Lord who goes before His people sword in hand. The Psalms tell us that He can be terrible to all who would touch those who are 'the apple of His eye'. How awe-inspiring are the prophecies with regard to Babylon by whose rivers God's people sat down and wept. All these predictions had their fulfilment. Babylon was blotted out for ever both for its pride and for its lack of mercy and sympathy toward the suffering people of God whom it had brought into captivity.

To all the people of God, life in retrospect is a miracle of His preserving mercy and power. We look back and bow our heads, as with thankfulness we say with David:

> *Unless the Lord had been my help*
> *When I was sore opprest,*
> *Almost my soul had in the house*
> *Of silence been at rest.*

God is here also spoken of as the Lover of His people. 'For the Lord hath chosen Jacob for himself, and Israel for his peculiar treasure.' 'Jacob have I loved.' This is a sovereign love of which all who belong to Christ make a personal discovery. 'We love him because he first loved us.'

One of the greatest tragedies of our fallen world is to see men who were created to glorify God worshipping false or dead 'gods'. 'They that make them are like unto them.' The sweetest drop in our cup of blessing is the spiritual desire to worship the One who alone should command our love. 'Praise the Lord; for the Lord is good: sing praises unto his name; for it is pleasant.'

PSALM 138: REVIVAL

'Though I walk in the midst of trouble, Thou wilt revive me'

It is in the day of trouble that our cries go up to God for help. It was in his night of trouble that Jacob wrestled with the Angel of the Covenant and was revived and blessed by God's presence and promise. It was in the furnace of fire that the three young men in Babylon were preserved by the Brother who was born for adversity. It was while tossed in the storm that the cry of the disciples awaked their Lord out of sleep. In the path of trouble David, like Paul, learned that nothing would ever emerge in his life but God's grace would be sufficient for him. 'My grace is sufficient for thee, for my strength is made perfect in weakness.' How often do we, in much fear, envisage the hour of our departure from this world! But listen: 'Yea, though I walk through the valley of the shadow of death, I will fear no evil: for thou art with me.' And if God be for us [and with us] who can be against us?

One Sabbath morning, many years ago, I was present in a certain home. It was the summer Communion season, and people were coming long distances to honour the solemn occasion. Before we sat down to conduct family worship a young man walked in. He had travelled many miles to be present at the service. Although he looked very sad, those present who knew his worth handed him the Bible and asked him to read. With a deep sigh he read part of a Psalm:

> *This word of thine my comfort is*
> *In mine affliction:*
> *For in my straits I am revived*
> *By this thy word alone.*

That same evening, as we walked together along a quiet road, we could both say, 'Did not our heart burn within us, while He talked with us by the way, and while

He opened to us the Scriptures?' The morning clouds appeared to have passed away. At eventide it was light. Shortly afterwards he was translated to the house of many mansions to be for ever with the Lord.

There was another day when I stood by the bed of a dying Christian man. These same words, formerly read in my hearing by my young friend, I also read there and sang. The Lord was with us, and our aged friend was revived and comforted by God's precious Word. With this staff in his hand he was about to cross his Jordan to possess his inheritance above. His day of trouble was almost over, to return no more.

### PSALM 139: 'THOU ART THERE'

Many a time have I stood in various pulpits and given out, as the custom was, the opening verses of this Psalm. The excellent men present would then arise 'to speak to the Question', or, in other words, to relate before the large congregations present some aspect of their Christian experience. Many, indeed, are the memories which I associate with this Psalm.

I knew, for example, a man who once walked along a lonely road. One of his deep-seated 'phobias' was a fear of isolation or loneliness, and this fear surfaced within him as he walked along that country road. Then he began to think of the words of this Psalm. 'Wherever I am,' he mused, 'God is beside me. "Thou art there." Yes, Lord, and Thou art here now. Thy blessed Spirit is with me, and, I hope, within me too.

Thine omniscient eye is upon me every step of the way, and Thy kindly hand is leading me always. The walls of Thy people are ever before Thee. Thy people were known to Thee before they were brought into existence. Thou knewest them in the womb, and they shall be known to Thee for ever.' As his fear left him he could not but bless Him who said, 'Lo, I am with you alway'.

Once I stood with a number of friends on a railway station in Glasgow. A devoted Christian nurse was on the eve of leaving us to labour on a mission-field in one of the distant places of the earth. She was to travel across both sea and land. The long journey into the unknown brought a measure of anxiety into her heart. As we bade one another a fond farewell I quoted an appropriate verse from this Psalm:

> *Take I the morning wings, and dwell*
> *In utmost parts of sea;*
> *Ev'n there, Lord, shall thy hand me lead,*
> *Thy right hand hold shall me.*

The words brought comfort to us all, and especially to the Lord's handmaid.

The greatest joy in the life of any man is to know this God who knows us. To know God savingly is to love Him. When Peter stood before the all-seeing One, who knew what was in his heart, he said, 'Lord, thou knowest all things, thou knowest that I love thee'.

It will not be long before those who love Him will, as on the wings of a dove, be taken to be with Him where He is. This was His own prayer on earth: 'Father, I will that they also, whom thou hast given me, be with me where I am.' How little we know of what happens in the moment of death! Our souls immediately pass into God's presence. Absent from the body we shall be present with the Lord. The beginning of bliss eternal!

PSALMS 140–141: THE DAY OF BATTLE
'Thou hast covered my head in the day of battle'

The second sight we get of David in the Scriptures is in his encounter with Goliath, the giant of Gath. While thousands of the 'mighty men' of Israel stood in fear before this massive, arrogant and well-armed man, David, conscious that God was his shield and his salvation, engaged him without fear in battle. With a sling in his hand, and his body unprotected by any visible armour, he faced the pagan giant who had defied the God of the armies of Israel. The Name of Jehovah was David's 'strong tower'. This immortal incident, as well as others in his life, was, we believe, in David's mind when he uttered these words.

Some of us have no experience of the terrors of physical warfare; but we have come across godly men who have, over a long period of time, been engaged in it, and whose lives God has shielded to the end. Yet deliverance from death is not invariably granted. Others, equally godly, have been struck down on the field of battle or have sunk into a watery grave.

'Thou hast covered my head in the day of battle': in the highest sense these words have to do with the spiritual warfare in which all God's people are engaged on earth. None of them is immune from Satan's arrows and fiery darts, or from the hatred of a godless world. God's spiritual armour, however, is adequate and invincible, no matter how hard and prolonged our conflicts may be. Significant, indeed, is the word 'thou' in this verse. God Himself was David's covering. 'Fear not, Abram; I am thy shield.'

There are some, as we know, whose conflicts are more severe than those of others. Paul, for example, had, by God's wise ordering, been led into depths of spiritual distress, that he might know how to minister comfort to those who had to pass through similar trials. 'Blessed be God . . . who comforteth us in all our tribulation, that we may be able to comfort them which are in any trouble, by the comfort wherewith we ourselves are comforted of God.' How reassuring also are his words, 'There hath no temptation taken you but such as is common to man: but God is faithful, who will not suffer you to be tempted above that ye are able; but will with the temptation also make a way to escape, that ye may be able to bear it'! How often in our own days of conflict have we turned to such books as Bunyan's *Grace Abounding to the Chief of Sinners*, Guthrie's *The Christian's Great Interest*, or to a biography of men like Spurgeon or J. C. Philpot? But, 'hitherto hath the Lord helped us'.

> *His feathers shall thee hide; thy trust*
> *Under his wings shall be:*
> *His faithfulness shall be a shield*
> *And buckler unto thee.*

God would have us comfort His people in anticipation of the day when their warfare shall be accomplished, and for ever at an end.

### PSALMS 142–143: DAYS OF OLD
'I remember the days of old'

In the midst of all his sorrows David could not but recall calmer and kinder days. He could remember the days when, as a shepherd lad, he sat by the flowing brook and watered the flock. These were days when God's peace filled his heart. The Shepherd of Israel led him by quiet waters and in pastures green. Spiritually speaking, he was still but a lamb of God's flock. The storms of life had not as yet broken in upon his life. Now, in his many afflictions, he could not but 'remember the days of old'. When Job was in great distress, he remembered the time when God's 'candle' shone upon his head and when the rays of divine light illumined his way. Naomi could recall similar days before God put the waters of Marah into her cup. 'Call me not Naomi [or pleasant], but call me Marah [or bitter]; for the Almighty hath dealt very bitterly with me.'

Have not all of us our wistful memories of other days? We remember when we first tasted that the Lord is gracious; the time of our spiritual rebirth when the Lord led us into His banqueting-house with His banner of love over us. We call to mind seasons of unusual nearness to Christ. And at times we are much inclined to say with the godly William Cowper:

> *Where is the blessedness I knew*
> *When first I saw the Lord?*
> *Where is the soul-refreshing view*
> *Of Jesus and His Word?*

We recall hours of fellowship with Christian friends, or times of refreshing when alone with the Lord. We remember beloved friends in Christ who are now in their eternal Home, 'far from a world of grief and sin, with Christ eternally shut in'.

Yes, these days are gone; but better days are yet to come! This is the meaning of David's prayer. 'Thou art my God: Thy Spirit is good; lead me into the land of uprightness.' I often think of an evening I once spent in Glasgow. An eminent minister of Christ – the late William Cameron of Resolis – preached a wonderful sermon on these words. It was a message which brought unspeakable comfort to many hearts. 'The land of uprightness' is 'where the inhabitant shall not say, I am sick', and where the afflictions mentioned in these Psalms are unknown. God shall wipe away all tears from our eyes. Our sighs shall be turned into songs. The years of our mourning shall be ended. As some of us moved away from the church that evening we felt that we had enjoyed something which would sustain us for many days.

'Happy is that people whose God is the Lord'

Martin Luther used to say that true religion is to be found in the personal pronouns. Often is this truth emphasized in this Book of Psalms. David frequently addressed his Redeemer as his own God. 'My God.' The voice of the Church in every age is, 'My Beloved is mine.' The most blessed hour in the life of Thomas was when, at his Lord's request, he looked at His nail-pierced hands and placed his trembling hand on the wounds in His side. 'My Lord and my God.' From that moment his unbelief was slain and he knew something more of the unspeakable love of the One who died for him. His was 'joy unspeakable and full of glory'.

'There is no joy,' says Augustine, in speaking of the soul's enjoyment of God, 'like the joy of those who love thee for thine own sake, whose joy thou thyself art.' Pascal, one of his great successors in the Apostolic faith, reminds us that 'happiness can never be found in ourselves or in external things, but in God and in ourselves as united to Him. If man is not made for God, how is it that he can be happy only in God alone?' All God's people, from the beginning of time, are in this way our spiritual contemporaries, and shall be to the end.

An excellent Christian woman once told me of a certain day when, while engaged in her domestic work, God's presence broke in upon her soul. All she could do was to fall down on her knees and repeat the words, 'My Lord and my God'. Her soul was transported into another and blissful world. It was an experience which refreshed her spirit for many days. My late old friend, Alexander MacAskill of Drynoch in Skye, often told about the day when, as he was walking on his native heath, God's love and presence took possession of his soul and these same words made him stand still. 'My Lord and my God.' How often would his eyes fill as he told his friends in the Lord about one of his Bethel hours!

We could spend many hours thinking of the unspeakably precious words which describe the different relationships in which Christ stands to His people – 'my God', 'my Redeemer', 'my Portion', 'my Beloved', 'my Friend', 'my Shepherd'. But this subject is too vast and too rich for us. In eternity we ever make new discoveries of Him whose love passes knowledge. 'Happy is that people that is in such a case: yea, happy is that people whose God is the Lord.'

PSALM 145: THE TRUE APOSTOLIC SUCCESSION

'One generation shall praise thy works to another, and shall declare thy mighty acts'

As there is a true apostolic succession within the Church of God, there is also an apostate succession which parades its blasphemous and unscriptural pretentions before a blind world. The papal system, for example, and all the negations and heresies of so-called modern Christianity, are expressive of an apostasy amazing in its depth. These two 'successions' have, in one form or another, existed in the world from the days of Abel and Cain. The one has scriptural consistency; the other never comes to the knowledge of the truth. The one is the faith once delivered to the saints; the other is a plethora of false 'dreams' woven by false prophets out of their own darkened minds. The one has the promise of preservation and victory; the other is doomed to destruction. Indeed, there is nothing in history more impressive than the survival of the true Church of God amidst all the hostilities of men and all the imitations of the truth which Satan brings on the scene. God's 'truth endureth to all generations'. 'His kingdom is an everlasting kingdom.' The Gospels provide us with a wonderful genealogical chain extending from Adam to Christ the Mediator, who binds together Jews and Gentiles, and who is the 'chief corner stone', the King and Head of His Church.

This chain has continued unbroken since the apostolic age. Men like Athanasius, Augustine, Luther, Calvin, and many others, have handed down this great heritage from generation to generation. And witnesses to the same truth shall be in our world to the end of time. Praise His Name!

The one theme of such men is God's revelation of Himself and His purposes in His infallible Word. How gloriously is this brought before us in this Psalm! It speaks of what God is, what God gives, and what God does. His mighty acts within the spheres of grace and providence are both merciful and 'terrible'. His people are all the subjects of His unchangeable love, but those who persist in their sins, though now in a room of mercy, shall one day come under His never-ending rebuke!

Christ commanded His messengers to preach the Gospel to every creature. He commanded all His people to pray the Lord of the harvest that He would send forth labourers into His harvest. May we be of those who fear Him and who display the banner of truth in our own day.

There is a sphere of labour where we may all begin, namely, our own hearths. 'Tell ye your children of it, and let your children tell their children, and their children another generation.'

### PSALMS 146–147: THE GREAT PHYSICIAN

'He healeth the broken in heart, and bindeth up their wounds'

In these two Psalms Christ, the Great Physician, is spoken of as the One whose power to heal is absolute over both soul and body. Millions of men and women who have known the deadly malady of sin shall stand at last without fault before His throne. The moment they die the souls of believers pass into heaven, and their bodies, which are sown in corruption, shall be raised up in incorruption and glory. 'I am the Lord who healeth thee.'

On earth our Lord manifested His power to heal, and to save 'to the uttermost'. I once heard an eminent Professor of Medicine say that we could bring all the medical skill in the world to the bedside of a dying man, but that there was 'a point of no return', when nothing could be done and the most skilful of friends were rendered helpless. But it was not so with Christ. Death, and 'all manner of diseases', He overcame by His touch and word. The blind received their sight, the lame walked, the lepers were cleansed, the bowed-down and the demon-possessed were released from their chains. No bruised reed did He ever break, or fail to make whole. And the health which He gave was everlasting. The physical manifestations of His power were the external evidences that His power had reached the soul also. These tokens of His power preceded and heralded the complete and final redemption of their entire beings.

Once I called on a beloved friend. He knew that he was dying. Both his lungs were in the grip of a fatal disease, but he was happy beyond words. With his hand over his chest he whispered, 'I shall be whole when I awake in the resurrection'. 'I shall be satisfied when I awake in thy likeness.'

Even the prospect of death should comfort us when we relate that solemn event to God's promise and to the Christian hope. 'For we know that if our earthly house of this tabernacle were dissolved, we have a building of God, an house not made with hands, eternal in the heavens.' Who can envisage that glorious day awaiting all the redeemed when 'mortality shall be swallowed up of life'?

'Praise him with the timbrel and dance'

These last Psalms bring us to the portals of bliss. The notes of sorrow which pervaded so many of the others are not found in these. 'The winter is past, the rain is over and gone; . . . the time of the singing of birds is come, and the voice of the turtle is heard in our land.' The great and terrible wilderness, with all its trials and dangers, is now behind heaven's pilgrim. The land of Beulah, with its sweet music and indescribable peace, he has now entered. All he now desires is to be for ever with the Lord in the great congregation above where praise will be perfected. Those who know something of the spiritual experiences which this incomparably precious Book brings before us will at last share in the joys awaiting the elect.

Throughout the long years of his ministry in Dingwall, Dr John Kennedy gave devotional comments on the Book of Psalms at the weekly Prayer Meeting. When he came to its end some felt that he himself was rapidly maturing for the kingdom of glory. And so it proved. The end of his life on earth coincided with solemn but joyous comments on these last Psalms.

Mary Fletcher, whose husband was one of the choice evangelical ministers of England in his day, was a lady who enjoyed much nearness to the Lord. Some might describe her as a 'mystical' lady, for she often recorded the wonderful communications of the Lord's mind to her soul 'in the night watches'. Some of her friends in the Lord were often blessed in a similar manner. In her Diary she records, for example, the dream of one of her friends. In his dream he saw himself in heaven among an innumerable company of angels and the spirits of just men made perfect; but it was the sight he enjoyed of Christ 'that filled his soul with joy inexpressible. Beams of glory proceeded from our Lord and touched every one of the glorified spirits, showing how all their glory proceeded from their union with the Supreme Good. His ecstasy was now great; he cried out and shouted the name of Jesus till he awoke. For three days he scarcely knew where he was – his soul was so wrapt up in the heavenly vision.'

But our hope of heaven does not rest on any such experiences as these, however precious they may be. Paul did not base his hope of being with God in glory on his wonderful hour in the third heaven where he saw and heard things of unspeakable wonder. His hope and comfort was based on the merits and finished work of Christ. 'This is a faithful saying and worthy of all acceptation, that Jesus Christ came into the world to save sinners, of whom I am chief.' The disciples on the mount of transfiguration had a glimpse of the infinite and enrapturing glory of their Lord. They also heard the voice which said, 'This is my Beloved Son in whom I am well pleased'. We have also a more sure word of prophecy; 'whereunto ye do well that ye take heed, as unto a light that shineth in a dark place, until the day dawn and the day star arise in your hearts'.

As we come to the end of this Book we know that we stand on the threshold of a world of which we know only in part. 'We know not yet what we shall be but we know that when he shall appear, we shall be like him, for we shall see him as he is.' 'The half was not told me.' 'Eye hath not seen, nor ear heard, neither have entered into the heart of man the things which God hath prepared for them that love him.'

'Let the children of Zion be joyful in their King. Let the saints be joyful in glory.'

AMEN and AMEN

M. Maclean.

June 1983.